WALES AFTER 1536
— A GUIDE

Wales After 1536
— a Guide

by
Donald Gregory

Dedication to:
Friends both sides of Offa's Dyke

ISBN: 0-86381-318-6

Cover: Anne Lloyd Morris

*First published in 1995 by Gwasg Carreg Gwalch,
Iard yr Orsaf, Llanrwst, Gwynedd, Wales.*

☎ *(01492) 642031*

Printed and Published in Wales

By the same author:

Wales Before 1066
Wales Before 1536
Country Churchyards in Wales
Radnorshire — A Historical Guide
Yesterday in Village Church and Churchyard (Gomer Press)

Portraits on cover:

William Morgan
Howell Harris
Gruffydd Jones
Hugh Williams

Contents

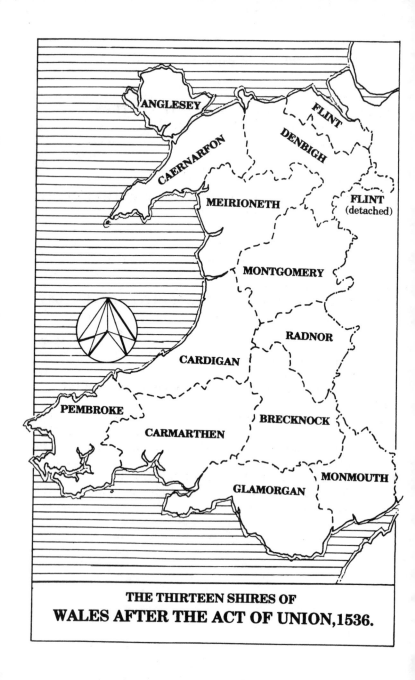

THE THIRTEEN SHIRES OF
WALES AFTER THE ACT OF UNION, 1536.

Foreword — Welsh Hopes and Fears

With the passing of the Act of Union in 1536 Wales became a part of England, the text of the *treaty* openly speaking of "annexation". Henry VIII however thought to sugar the pill by explaining to the Welsh that the Act would give them equality with the English and the same opportunities to advance themselves. Indeed it appears that most Welsh people accepted this royal assurance, bearing in mind that the King's own father, a Welshman, had won the Battle of Bosworth and captured the throne of England.

In 1542, six years after the political union of the two countries, a subsequent act of parliament announced the suzerainty of the laws of England at every level of Welsh life and made arrangements for the setting up in every Welsh county of local courts of Quarter Sessions, which, meeting four times a year, would be empowered to deal with every breach of the law of England, short of the most serious crimes of robbery and murder, which were to come under the aegis of higher courts, for which purpose Wales was divided up into four circuits, to be visited twice a year by Judges in Assize. (These so-called Great Sessions were to last until 1830.) Furthermore this act of parliament also insisted that in these courts of law, both Quarter Sessions, presided over by Justices of the Peace, and higher courts, where Judges held sway, only the English language would be tolerated. Farsighted Welshmen thereafter realised that those who wished to prosper in the new political climate would do well not only to learn English but also to speak it at every opportunity. In consequence the anglicisation of Wales proceeded apace, increasing the likelihood that in the course of time the Welsh language might become the language of only the unambitious and the underprivileged.

The intention of government in England after 1536 was clearly to treat Wales in every respect as a part of England, completely ignoring crucial differences in culture and in the Welsh pattern of historical development. At the same time this transition seems to have been sufficiently gradual for most Welshmen to be unaware of any significant change, apart from the obvious exclusion of the Welsh language from the courts of law.

Readers will observe that the last sections of all four parts of this book are called 'NOTES AND ILLUSTRATIONS'. The author claims the indulgence of purists for these Notes while he seeks to entertain other readers with anecdotes, biographical data and other perhaps irrelevant but not uninteresting historical material.

A
Part 1. Religion in the 16th Century

a. The Reformation in Wales (1535-1558)

In the early years of the 16th century came the Reformation, the break-away of a considerable part of Europe from the authority of Rome, which in the Middle Ages had shared power with the Holy Roman Empire, the Emperor for the most part ruling men's bodies while the Pope made himself responsible for their minds. This dichotomy was to be fractured at the beginning of the 16th century, but, whereas on the mainland of Europe the Reformation was initially caused by the religious teaching of the German monk, Martin Luther, there was an altogether different set of circumstances operating on this side of the Channel. For, despite the fact that from the time of John Wyclif in the 14th century, there had been growing resentment here of the continuing authority of Rome, what happened in the reign of Henry VIII had at first absolutely nothing at all to do with the religious ideas of Wyclif and Luther. Indeed Henry so disapproved of the revolutionary religious stand taken by Luther in 1517 that four years later he wrote a thorough denunciation of Luther's Protest, to which the newly-invented printing press was able to give much publicity. So very pleased was the Pope with this opposition to Luther that he rewarded Henry with the title of Defender of the Faith, (*Fidei Defensor*), the initials of which (*FD*), readers will hardly need reminding, still appear on our coins!

Between 1521 and 1527 however circumstances caused Henry to change his mind, not indeed about Luther's religious opposition to Rome, but about his own attitude to the authority of the Pope. Having grown tired of his wife, Catherine of Aragon, who had failed to produce a son, Henry wanted a divorce to enable him to marry the niece of the Duke of Norfolk, Anne Boleyn, with whom he had fallen in love. In 1527 his Chancellor, Thomas Wolsey was given the thankless task of petitioning the Pope for a divorce for his royal master, citing as justification the invalidity of Henry's

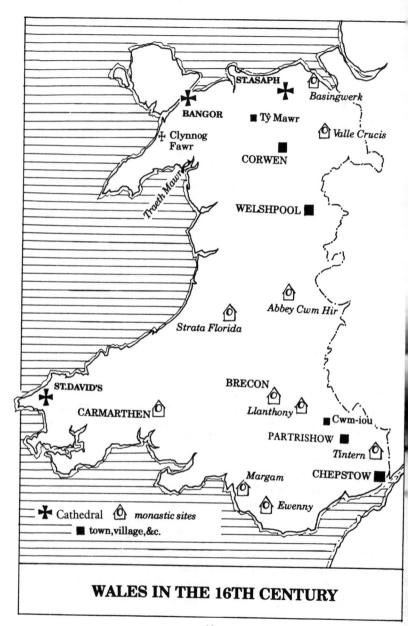

ST.ASAPH

Basingwerk

BANGOR

Tŷ Mawr

Valle Crucis

Clynnog
Fawr

CORWEN

Traeth Mawr

WELSHPOOL

Abbey Cwm Hir

Strata Florida

BRECON

ST.DAVID'S

CARMARTHEN

Llanthony

Cwm-iou

PARTRISHOW

Tintern

Margam

CHEPSTOW

Ewenny

✠ Cathedral   🏠 *monastic sites*
■ town, village, &c.

WALES IN THE 16TH CENTURY

marriage to Catherine, who at the time of their marriage, nearly a quarter of a century previously, was the newly-bereaved widow of Henry's elder brother. Arthur, who had died in 1502. (In taking this line Henry was conveniently forgetting that Catherine's second marriage had at the time received an official dispensation from the Vatican!) In 1529, after two years of deliberation, Pope Clement VII decided against a divorce for Henry VIII.

In the same year Henry, throwing caution to the winds, called Parliament, which thereafter for seven eventful years piecemeal brought about a complete break with Rome. Two men, from different backgrounds and with different objects, served the royal will. Thomas Cranmer, already at variance with Roman on religious matters, was made Archbishop of Canterbury in 1533, while Thomas Cromwell became Henry's political henchman. Every year from 1529 Parliament made inroads into papal power; in 1533 the parliamentary veto on all appeals to Rome was followed by the King's order to Cranmer to try his divorce case. The divorce was of course speedily granted, Henry's first marriage to the Spanish Catherine being declared invalid. The King, who had already secretly married Anne Boleyn, at once had her crowned Queen. The tie with Rome was thus broken; parliamentary approval came the next year with the passage of the Act of Supremacy, which explicitly stated that the King was the supreme head of the Church of England, to which the Pope's predictable retort was to excommunicate Henry and declare him deposed. Thus the first, the political part of the Reformation was brought about here, but any changes in religious beliefs were not at this stage being contemplated. Readers will please bear in mind that the Act of Union, whereby Wales became joined to England, was to follow the next year, 1536.

Wales thus on the morrow of the Act of Union found itself part and parcel of a country which had severed its ties with Roman Catholicism; such changes as took place in religious practice in church thereafter were to affect churches in Wales as much as in England. It would be misleading however to give the impression that churchgoers in Wales greatly resented such changes as took place in the services they attended; indeed it is very probable that the changeover in Wales was smoother than it was in England, but this was not however to be ascribed to any great enthusiasm shown by the Welsh for Henry's volte-face. It has to be remembered that before the Reformation in Wales services were conducted in Latin, of which most worshippers had no knowledge at all. After the passage of the Act of Supremacy Latin was superseded by English, a language which was as incomprehensible to most Welshmen at this time as Latin had been. The substitution of the Protestant prayer-book for the Roman Catholic missal made little difference to those who understood neither tongue. The Reformation thus could hardly in early days have been expected to stir up much Welsh enthusiasm when it amounted to little more than an English priest reading to a Welsh congregation from an English Bible. When, in 1534, following the passage through Parliament of the Act of Supremacy, all the clergy in England and Wales were required to recognise the King as the Supreme Head of the Church of England, only two priests in the whole of Wales in fact refused, and neither of them was a Welshman!

Thomas Cromwell's ambitions for his royal master went far beyond putting him at the head of his own church and thus independent of the spiritual authority of Rome; he fully shared Henry's intention of making himself the powerful ruler of a modern state and in order to achieve this position of strength he would need greatly to replenish the exchequers of state. Hence Cromwell directed Henry's willing attention to the monasteries whose assets would be so helpful in financing the powerful nation state which he envisaged. It has to be realised that these monasteries, which had in past centuries served medieval society very well indeed in a wide variety of ways, had by this 16th century fallen on bad times and in many cases were already in an advanced state of decay, with however many of their secular assets largely unimpaired.

Between 1536 and 1540 all houses of religion in England and Wales were suppressed, their priors and abbots driven from their places, to be severely punished if they resisted the change or pensioned off, if they were lucky. Of the forty-six such establishments in Wales, dissolved by the King in the 1530s, the best known ones on the eve of their dissolution were the Augustinian priory at Llanthony in the Honddu Valley, the Benedictine abbeys at Chepstow and at Usk, and the Cistercian monasteries at Abbey Cwm Hir in remotest Radnorshire, Basingwerk, Margam, Neath, Strata Florida, Tintern and Vallé Crucis, while the Benedictine abbey at Ewenny was saved by being incorporated into the Priory there and the abbey at Brecon became the nucleus of the future cathedral. Some details of the subsequent fate of former abbeys, at Tintern, Strata Florida and Llanthony will be found in a later part of this section of the book, under 'Notes and Illustrations'.

Once the personnel in the monasteries had been dealt with, the lands and wealth were taken over by the royal commissioners, who redistributed these very considerable assets in ways that were most favourable for the advancement of the King's plans for power. There seems to have been virtually no outcry in Wales at what seems to us to have been a policy of ruthless exploitation; there was some Welsh resentment, though not of any real significance, when later in the 1530s much-loved images were destroyed and time-honoured religious pilgrimages were forbidden.

At the same time that the King was divorcing Catherine of Aragon and was beginning to pursue wider ambitions to make himself a powerful monarch, an ambition much favoured and advanced by Thomas Cromwell, there was also a growing undercurrent of Protestantism in the country, the source of which had sprung from the preaching in the second half of the 14th century of John Wyclif, an Oxford scholar, who was Master of Balliol; he had begun by condemning what he saw as the corruption of the Pope, later moving on to deny the validity of some parts of Catholic doctrine before virtually challenging the supreme authority, claimed by the Pope. The spiritual inheritors of Wyclif's way of thinking in the 1530s took advantage of the opportunity afforded by the King's break with Rome. In 1537 and 1538 these Protestant leanings revealed themselves; in the former year a religious manual, known as the Bishop's Book, written by Thomas Cranmer, the Archbishop of Canterbury, himself a man of Protestant tendencies, was circulated among the clergy. This was followed in 1538 by the placing — and chaining — in every parish church in the land of a copy of a new English translation of the Bible, based on the work of the Protestant Tyndale. This was the so-called Great Bible, that Shakespeare knew. One consequence of this preaching of the Bible was, in the words of G.M. Trevelyan, that "men could read the Bible and think what they liked in silence". Henry VIII, for his part, soon sensed the dangers implicit in these acts and quickly put a stop to what to his way of thinking was Protestant heresy.

In 1539 a newly-elected and extremely servile Parliament meekly accepted from the King a statement of his own religious views, incorporated in the so-called Six Articles, and proceeded to pass an Act which threatened draconian penalties against those who failed to observe its provisions, amongst which were the enforcement of celibacy among all clergy, and an absolute ban on speaking or writing against transubstantiation. This year, 1539, represented the high water mark of Henry's despotic powers; it was the year in which a man was burned to death for eating meat on a Friday. It was also the year when Thomas Cromwell talked Parliament into accepting the monstrous notion that any royal proclamation was to have the force of law. Cromwell, having loaded his master with despotic powers, himself suffered from their application in 1540, when, arrested on a trumped-up charge, he was speedily beheaded.

In the last five years of Henry's reign, from 1542 to 1547, the King tended to mark time, as he tried to consolidate his position; in one respect at least he showed an unusual impartiality, as he sent to the block both Catholics and Protestants, the former for questioning his claim to religious supremacy, the latter for disagreeing with his theology. At his death in 1547 England and Wales remained Catholic in doctrine, a state of affairs, which in Wales at any rate was greeted with complete apathy. The time was still far in the future when Wales was to become by far the most Protestant part of the United Kingdom.

The widespread apathy in Wales, which had attended most of the religious changes in Henry's reign, became tinged with resentment in the reign of Edward VI, the boy-king who ruled from 1547 to 1553 under the successive Protectorships of the Dukes of Somerset and Northumberland. England became a strictly Protestant country during those six years, when significant changes in doctrine were accompanied by more superficial but much more obvious practical measures, such as the despatch of royal commissioners from London to all parts, their instructions to destroy chantries, confiscate surviving religious endowments, and even to knock down images, crosses and altars, which apparently reminded extreme Protestants of Roman Catholicism.

Fortunately for those in Wales who treasured their altars and their churchyard crosses, some of these churches, which housed these honoured relics, were in remote places, a long, long way from London. As confirmation of the survival of some of these objects readers are advised to visit Partrishow in Gwent (GR 279224); the old church (there is no other building in the neighbourhood) is four and a half miles north east of Crickhowell, and contains several stone altars, which bear on their tops a number of incised consecration crosses, while in the churchyard still stands in its original height a medieval cross, the King's commissioners having totally failed to find their way to this idyllic spot.

To summarise Protestant activity in Edward's reign, the foundations of the tyrannical government of Henry VIII were successfully undermined, when the harsh laws of 1539 were repealed. Thereafter full legislative power was restored to Parliament. In 1549 the First Prayer Book of Edward VI, the work of Cranmer, was imposed on the church, to be replaced three years later, by the Second Prayer Book, which is basically the same prayer book which is still in use in the Church of England today. In 1553 England and Wales officially embraced Protestantism when Protestant beliefs were defined in the Forty-Two Articles, but in the summer of that year the sickly Edward died, and the crown passed to his half-sister, Mary, daughter of the Roman Catholic Catherine of Aragon, whom Henry VIII had spurned.

To the English the volte-face of the years of Mary's reign, (1553-1558) brought horror or rejoicing according to individual religious beliefs, whereas to most ordinary Welsh people the apathy with which they had met the many changes they had known since the annexation of their land by England continued as Protestantism was abandoned by Mary's Parliament and Roman Catholicism restored. Remember that to the Welsh the Roman Catholic missal, which was in use until rejected by Protestants, and the Protestant Prayer Book, introduced in Edward VI's reign and the former Catholic missal restored again by Mary were both written in alien and largely incomprehensible tongues.

The barebones of Mary's reign are these. She succeeded her half-brother, Edward in 1553; the thirty-seven year old daughter of Henry VIII, Mary was personally popular, her succession being widely welcomed by the general public until it became clear that she was more sympathetic towards her mother's country, Spain, than she was towards her own. It has to be stressed that Spain, having been of late marvellously enriched by the silver her successful sailors had brought home from the New World, was developing alarming political amibitions in Europe. In 1554 Mary married the Spanish king's son, Philip, who became King of Spain in 1556, when Charles V abdicated from the throne of Spain. Thereafter until Mary's death in 1558 England became virtually a vassal of Spain.

Parliament carried out the Queen's wishes and repealed all the anti-Catholic laws with the result that the Pope regained his previous spiritual supremacy in this country. Between 1555 and 1558 three hundred Protestants were burned at the stake in England, including Cranmer, Latimer and Ridley, who perished in Oxford in 1555; in Wales however only three Protestants suffered in this way, of whom the most prominent was Robert Farrer, the Bishops of St Davids, who met his fate in Carmarthen.

Despite the widespread apathy in Wales towards the various religious changes of these times, there were of course among the educated minority a number of devout men of religion (almost all of whom were educated at Oxford) who put their religious consciences, be they Catholic or Protestant, before their professional advancement. There seem not to have been any Vicars of Bray in Wales! Two outstanding Protestants were Richard Davies and Rowland Meyrick; the former, of humble birth, the son of a curate in the Conwy Valley, went to Oxford, where he became attracted to the prevailing revolutionary talk of young Protestants. After leaving the university he became a priest but on Mary's accession in 1553, after being summoned to appear before the Privy Council, was deprived of his living. He then exiled himself and his family to Frankfurt until Mary died. More will be heard of this distinguished priest and scholar in Elizabeth's reign. Rowland Meyrick, who, like Davies, became a Protestant at Oxford, in 1550 had been made Canon and Precentor of St David's until he was forced out of office by Mary in 1553.

In the other religious camp were three determined and devout Catholics, Morys Clynnog, Morgan Phillips and Gruffydd Robert. Morys Clynnog, born in Clynnog Fawr in 1525, after studying theology at Oxford, became Rector of Corwen in 1556; early in 1558 he was appointed Bishop of Bangor but before he could be consecrated, Queen Mary died and Morys Clynnog fled voluntarily into exile. Morgan Phillips, a son of South Wales, after graduating at Oxford, succeeded Rowland Meyrick as Precentor of St David's in 1553 on Mary's accession. He stayed in St David's until her reign ended when he fled to the continent. Most important of Welsh Catholics at this time was Gruffydd Robert; born in Caernarfonshire in 1522, he was educated at Oxford, being appointed in 1558 Archdeacon of Anglesey but had to flee soon afterwards. He was one of the most distinguished Welsh figures in the Renaissance, being a poet, a song-writer and a scholar as well as being a priest. His book on Welsh grammar is regarded as a masterpiece of clear writing, which did a great deal in the Renaissance years to elevate the Welsh language as a medium of educated expression. He was one of the great grammarians of Wales.

b. The Elizabethan Settlement

With the death of Mary in the summer of 1558, it was all change again; in eleven years the country had known four rulers, a ruthless father and his three children, the father, who had changed his religion solely for political reasons, having been followed by a sickly, underage son, whose guardians had made the most of their opportunity to adopt extreme Protestant policies. On Edward's death the pendulum had swung back again, welcoming the Pope back to England and restoring Roman Catholicism here. Five years later, in 1558, when Catholic Mary died, her half-sister Elizabeth, who succeeded her, was faced with the vexed problem of unravelling once and for all, if at all possible, the complicated religious tangle. This then was the first problem encountered by the twenty-five year old daughter of Anne Boleyn; however, unlike her half-brother and her half-sister, who had preceded her on the throne, Elizabeth had no strong religious beliefs of her own, a fortunate circumstance which made it possible for her to attempt to secure some sort of compromise. This she was determined at all costs to achieve.

The drastic religious upsets of recent years had been for the most part motivated by fanaticism, which, if it had continued into the new reign, could well have endangered national unity. This danger the young queen quickly realised, causing her from the very beginning of her reign to act with the greatest circumspection. Politically she found herself in a very exposed situation, as Spain was clearly in the ascendant and in order to make herself even more powerful was attempting to enter into an alliance with France, at a time when the heir to the throne of France had recently married Elizabeth's cousin, the Catholic Mary of Scotland, who was next in succession to the throne of England. Elizabeth on the very morrow of her accession was presented with the real possibility of having in the future to be opposed by a hostile alliance between Spain, France and Scotland. Meanwhile, despite the gravity of the international outlook, she had the good sense first to attend to the ever-pressing problems at home, posed by fundamental differences of religious opinion.

Elizabeth's troubles started at her coronation, when only one bishop was prepared to recognise the legitimacy of her succession; hence she was crowned by the Bishop of Carlisle. The Queen thereafter found it politically expedient to take heed of advice proffered by Protestants rather more than she had originally intended. Turning her attention at once to the religious issues that confronted her, she was shrewd enough not to repeat the mistake made by her father, Henry VIII, when he forced Parliament to give his personal edicts the force of law; instead Elizabeth arranged for the speedy free election of a new Parliament, to which she handed the problem of solving the religious dispute, though of course from time to time she attempted to steer the course of the long debate. Meanwhile the bishops, who had been one and all appointed by the dead Catholic Mary, stood their ground, both in the House of Lords and in the House of Convocation, where Elizabeth made no attempt to stop them from speaking their minds. Gradually, however, but surely, the bishops were worsted in debate by laymen. The settlement, when it emerged, was very much a laymen's settlement, reached only after long and earnest debate. It was not to be imposed by authority. When the bishops resolutely refused to accept the agreed changes, then and only then did the Queen act, by replacing them by men, who were very carefully chosen for their moderate, middle of the road, views.

The new religious order became law in April 1559, when Parliament passed two acts, the first of which was an Act of Supremacy, which for the second time abolished papal authority here; the accompanying legislation, an Act of Uniformity stated the doctrines and beliefs of the Church of England. The second Prayer Book of Edward VI was adopted with a number of minor modifications. This new Prayer Book was carefully worded to give as little offence as possible to Roman Catholics who might be wavering. Indeed it contained no specific criticism of Rome. This tactic proved successful in so far as many moderate Catholics did join the Church of England. Politically the settlement was a sensible compromise and it is perhaps significant that in the opening years of the new reign, up to 1565, there was no persecution of Catholics. Indeed in those years only two hundred clergy found themselves unable to give the necessary assurances and were deprived of their livings.

What has so far been said about Elizabeth's religious settlement of course affected everybody in England and Wales; nevertheless some readers may feel that this general account of events has too little direct relevance to Wales. It has however to be remembered that, whether it liked it or not, Wales had been subject to the laws of Westminster since 1536. Furthermore — and this may surprise some — at this time, that is to say, at the accession of Elizabeth, few Welshmen showed any dissatisfaction with the new arrangements made for their country's government. A great many Welshmen, those with land and education, were becoming very anglicised and had developed a vested interest in Tudor prosperity. The evil in the Act of Union, which largely arose from the ban on the use of the Welsh language in courts of law at all levels, had not as yet been fully felt.

On the morrow of the 1559 legislation official Visitors were appointed to the four dioceses of Wales in order to administer the oath of Supremacy to all the clergy and to make sure that the new Prayer Book was properly in circulation and in use. Of these official Visitors to Wales three men merit particular mention, all three were Welsh, Oxford-educated and were worthy representatives of the New Learning. Rowland Meyrick, who, it has already been seen, when Canon and Precentor of St David's, had been forced into exile by Mary, in 1559 was appointed Bishop of Bangor. Thomas Young, a Pembrokeshire man, and, like Meyrick, a former Precentor at St David's, had also gone into exile in Mary's reign; in January 1560 Elizabeth made him Bishop of St David's, the premier ecclesiastical office in Wales, before elevating him to the see of York in the following year. Third of this distinguished trio was Richard Davies. A man of the Conwy Valley, he had in the middle 1550s shown himself so fervent a Protestant in the discharge of his religious duties that he had been hauled up before the Privy Council when Mary became Queen.

Richard Davies, who went into exile, was later to play an even more important part in the history of Wales.

In the event nothing much came out of the visitation to Wales; the reasons for a low-key reception seem complex. Most churchgoers had no opinion at all, the English prayer book meaning as little to them as the Latin missal. Of the others, many perhaps only paid lip-service, where they thought that the Elizabethan changes might have as short a life as those that preceded them in Henry VIII's reign, Edward VI's and in Mary's. On the other hand some will have welcomed with real relief an end to the bickering, while others were probably prepared to say anything to keep the peace. Of religious enthusiasm at this time there was little actual evidence, except in the cases of the handful of devout priests, who refused to toe the line, the most distinguished of whom, who have already been referred to in Mary's reign for their stalwart support of the old religion, were Gruffydd Robert, Morys Clynnog and Morgan Phillips, who all chose to go into exile; all three in later years, when the time seemed more propitious, were to play leading roles in planning the return of Roman Catholicism to Wales. In these early years of Elizabeth's reign too the young Queen, in marked contrast to her behaviour in later times, showed real tolerance towards those who disagreed with her in religious matters.

c. The Struggle for the Mind of Wales

Educated Welshmen by this time, whether Protestants or Roman Catholics, whether they lived in Wales or in exile in Europe, realised that the utter apathy of their fellow countrymen towards the drastic religious changes of the sixteenth century, could not be overcome until all Welshmen could hear their spiritual leaders talking to them in a language they could all understand. As the English had the very clear intention of lessening the use of Welsh rather than of encouraging it, it was up to the Welsh themselves to take the lead in the matter. On this crying need for books, written in Welsh, to be made available in order that ordinary Welsh people might be properly informed about religious matters of great moment, Protestants and Roman Catholics were for once in complete accord, each group believing that if only their message might reach ordinary people in Welsh, they would surely in consequence be able to see the light, as each denomination saw it.

Probably the first Welshman to see the need for religious books to be written in Welsh was William Salesbury, who, born about 1520, probably in Llansannan in Denbighshire, was educated at Maenan Abbey in the Conwy Valley (his father came from Llanrwst) before going on to study at Oxford, where he first decided that Wales above all needed the Bible to be translated into Welsh. Meanwhile in 1551 he published his own Welsh translation of the lessons, which were to be read in church; this worthy venture was unfortunately doomed to failure because Salesbury used such archaic and high-falutin' language that few of his hearers could understand what was being said. During Mary's reign, from 1553-58 he lay low, thereby escaping official action against him.

In 1561, by which time Elizabeth's new religious order was in place, word went forth from London that the lessons in Welsh churches should be read twice, first in English, then in Welsh; this edict helped to prepare the way for the welcome official announcement two years later of a parliamentary bill, which would arrange for the translation of the Bible and the Prayer Book into Welsh, although the period of three years allowed for this to happen was very over-optimistic.

This salutary parliamentary edict of 1563 was first heeded by Richard Davies, one of the four Visitors originally appointed by Elizabeth to see that her religious settlement was being carried out in Wales; appointed Bishop of St Asaph in 1559, he had been promoted in 1561 to St David's, from which see he wrote to William Salesbury, inviting him to collaborate with him in carrying out the official summons to translate the Bible and the Prayer Book into Welsh. Salesbury gladly accepted the offer and for two years the two scholars seem to have worked in reasonable partnership, completing the translating of the New Testament and the Prayer Book, with Salesbury apparently being chiefly responsible for the former and Davies for the latter.

The Prayer Book was very favourably received but Salesbury's translation of the New Testament, like his earlier attempt at translating lessons was largely incomprehensible to most ordinary Welsh people, with whom he seems to have had little real contact. Nevertheless the two men then turned their attention to translating the Old Testament, but, after a while, their efforts came to a full stop and the two scholars parted company. Common report had it that they had quarrelled bitterly over the translation of a single word, but modern scholars however tend to the belief that while serious differences of opinion did occur, financial considerations may have also played a considerable part. Thus this great and vital task was left unfinished with the result that ordinary Welsh Christians, as will be seen, were to have to wait another twenty years before being allowed access to the Bible in their own language.

William Salesbury has probably not been given his due by posterity; after all he had been the first man to realise the great need for a Welsh Bible. It was his misfortune — and that of his fellow Welshmen — that he failed to possess the necessary common touch. Nevertheless he did perform another very useful service to Wales in compiling an English-Welsh dictionary. Sir John Wynn, his contemporary and near neighbour in the Conwy Valley, called him "a Protestant humanist scholar and the chief representative of the Renaissance in Wales".

Meanwhile, while Bishop Davies and William Salesbury were busy at work with their translating, devoted scholars of the opposite, Roman Catholic persuasion, who were languishing in exile in Italy, were being equally industrious in pursuing their very different goals. Gruffydd Robert, who was probably the most important of Welsh Catholics, had already achieved a reputation for his Welsh scholarship, before being forced into exile. In 1564 he was appointed by the Pope to be Chaplain of the English Hospital in Rome, but soon was promoted to a position of much greater power and potential in Milan, where he stayed for twenty years in the service of the Cardinal Archbishop Borromeo. During these long years of exile he wrote, among other books, a Welsh grammar, on which much of his reputation as an outstanding Welsh scholar was based. Gruffydd Robert was a great Welsh patriot, who, apart from his devotion to the Roman Catholic faith and his desire to see Roman Catholicism restored to his native land, was also a fervent believer in the excellence of the Welsh language as a medium for the spread of Welsh culture.

Morys Clynnog, whose promotion in 1558 to the bishopric of Bangor was only prevented by the death of Queen Mary, was another very influential Welsh figure in Italian exile; in Rome in 1567 he wrote (in Welsh) an important treatise on Roman Catholic doctrine, while further north in the Netherlands, two more Welsh Roman Catholics, Morgan Phillips and Owen Lewis helped to set up in Douai a college for the training of Roman Catholic missionaries, whose future task would be to try to bring back the Roman Catholic faith to England and Wales.

The activities of devout Welsh Roman Catholics like Gruffydd Robert, Morys Clynnog and Morgan Phillips have to be seen as part and parcel of a great Roman Catholic attempt on the continent to restore the fortunes of the Roman Catholic church. By 1540 the Roman Catholic church had realised somewhat belatedly that their own house needed to be put in order before any large-scale attempt could be made to restore the fortunes of Roman Catholicism. In 1546 the Council of Trent was called with the twofold task assigned to it of cleaning up the church and of deciding ways and means of winning back those countries which had become Protestant.

Contemporary with the deliberations of the Council of Trent was the growth and development of the Society of Jesus, the Jesuits, an order of militant Catholics, founded in 1540 by Ignatius of Loyola, with the avowed purpose of opposing the further spread of Protestantism. By 1562 the members of the Council of Trent had finished their long years of soul-searching and had made their plans for the future, the instrument devised for the bringing back of back-sliders being the Inquisition. The widespread Catholic revival, which the Council of Trent set in motion was known as the

Counter Reformation. The political champion of this Counter Reformation, who was also the most powerful Catholic ruler in Europe, was Philip II of Spain, at a time when the chief champion of Protestantism was Elizabeth; after about 1560 these two countries, champions of two different religious faiths, were on a collision course. Thereafter war between Spain and England seemed inevitable.

The years 1569, 1570 and 1571 were years of great danger for England, years in which discontented Catholic aristocrats here encouraged the Catholic Mary, Queen of Scots to stake an illegal claim to the throne of England. The risings were numerous and sporadic and were easily put down but they caused Elizabeth to harden her heart against her Catholic subjects. Many a day was thereafter to elapse before religious tolerance returned to this country.

The Pope in 1570 retaliated in the face of Elizabeth's firm stand against Catholic plotters by excommunicating her and relieving all her Catholic subjects from their vows of allegiance to the Queen, who replied characteristically by declaring that in future she would treat all her subjects who remained Catholic as traitors. Four years later, in 1574, Roman Catholic missionaries, trained in Douai by Morgan Phillips, Owen Lewis and others crossed over from the Netherlands, the very first such missionary being a Welshman, Lewis Barlow, a Pembrokeshire man. In the following years a stream of missionaries followed from Douai, Rome and later from seminaries in Spain. Their efforts were greatly strengthened in 1580, when the Jesuits too sent their representatives here, of whom the best known, and the most saintly, was Edmund Campion. Parliament, thoroughly alarmed by this development, in 1581 passed an Act, which imposed a fine of £20 (an enormous sum of money in those days) on all who refused to attend their parish church.

As to Wales, there was certainly a marked increase in the amount of Catholic missionary activity in the late 1570s and the early 1580s both in the north and the south of the country but the rigorous imposition of penal laws and the growing fear of Spain (the Armada sailed in 1588) makes it impossible to quantify Catholic resurgence in Wales. What is known is that in the remaining years of Elizabeth's reign no fewer than one hundred and eighty seven recusants, as those Catholics were called, who failed to obey the law, were executed, but readers should not judge one century by the standards of another nor should they forget that between 1555 and 1558 no fewer than three hundred Protestants had also been executed, by Mary's orders.

During these anxious times of crisis and intolerance in the 1570s and 80s, in the quiet rural parish in Denbighshire of Llanrhaeadr-ym-Mochnant the vicar toiled away in his study month after month, year after year translating the Bible into Welsh. William Morgan, who had been born in 1545 at Tŷ Mawr, a farmhouse in the Wybrnant Valley, near Penmachno, was the son of a tenant of Sir John Wynn of Gwydir in the Conwy Valley, in whose house the promising young William was educated, before being sent to Cambridge. Subsequently he held livings at Llanbadarn Fawr and at Welshpool, moving to Llanrhaeadr in 1572. At Cambridge he had been encouraged by his tutor to turn his hand to translating religious books into Welsh; at Llanrhaeadr he found the chance and during his years there, from 1572 to 1587, William Morgan translated the Old Testament and re-translated the New, turning William Salesbury's stilted version into contemporary Welsh idiom. However, rightly or wrongly, voices began to be raised in the parish against what seemed to his critics to be time-wasting habits, voices which grew so loud that they reached the ears of John Whitgift, the Archbishop of Canterbury, who ordered Morgan to come to London to plead his case. Fortunately for the future of Welsh culture and Welsh Protestantism the Archbishop was wholly convinced and sent Morgan back home, comforted and encouraged to carry on with his great work, which he finished in 1587.

This Welsh Bible appeared in 1588, the year, be it remembered, when the Spanish dream of conquering England faded, as the Armada broke up on our inhospitable shores. Certainly Richard Davies and William Salesbury had played very important parts in furthering this great achievement but most of the credit has rightly been given to William Morgan. Indeed there are those who believe that this Welsh Bible of 1588 is the most important book ever to be written in Welsh, the same experts crediting Morgan with having thereby saved the Welsh language. Morgan did for Wales what Shakespeare did for England, and at about the same time; they both rendered respectable the languages in which they wrote. There was however a time-lag of forty years before ordinary Welsh people could read this Bible as Morgan's translation did not appear in a cheap — and therefore generally available — edition until 1630. Morgan himself was rewarded for his labours by being made Bishop of Llandaff in 1595 and six years later Bishop of St Asaph, where, according to Sir John Wynn's contemporary account, "he repaired and slated the chancel of the cathedral church, which was a great ruin".

d. The Beginnings of Non-Conformist Dissent

No village in Wales today is complete without a non-conformist chapel, thus presenting a very different picture from that of the sixteenth century, when there was no such place as a chapel of that kind. Nonconformity only began to take root in Wales in the middle of the seventeenth century, when in the short-lived Commonwealth of the 1650s Quakers and Baptists first openly expressed dissent in their places of worship. Methodism, readers are reminded, represents a later mode of dissent, the earliest such chapels in Wales being built in the first quarter of the nineteenth century, following the great missionary efforts of Howell Harris in the second half of the previous century. However, despite the almost total absence of any nonconformist activity in the sixteenth century, there was one lone dissenting voice raised in Wales, that of John Penry, crying in the Welsh wilderness; his unique, heroic — and quite ineffectual — contribution justifies inclusion in this chapter because he was a man of absolute integrity, who burned with a passionate desire to satisfy the spiritual needs of his under-privileged fellow Welshmen.

John Penry was born in 1563 into a Wales to which

Protestantism had only recently come in the trappings of the Church of England, whose priests read from an English Bible to their largely uncomprehending congregations. His home was in Brecknockshire, near Llangamarch, and he was educated at Christ College, Brecon and at Peterhouse, Cambridge. At Cambridge, where he studied theology, he came into contact with students, whose interest in the revolutionary ideas of the Puritans, attracted Penry, who spent most of his university vacations in Northampton, at that time a hotbed of Puritanism. He was entertained there by a Puritan family, the Godleys, whose daughter, Eleanor, he later married. He graduated in 1584 and after a spell in Oxford returned in 1586 to his home in Wales, where he withdrew for a while to write his first book, a short treatise, which was above all an impassioned plea to Elizabeth and her government to right, what according to him, were the many wrongs suffered by his fellow countrymen. Five hundred copies were printed and circulated in London, where to his chagrin John Penry was almost immediately arrested on the instructions of the Archbishop of Canterbury, John Whitgift.

He appeared before the Court of High Commission to answer charges of slandering the Government and committing treason and heresy, whereas in truth all he had had in mind was to draw the attention of the public to the many problems of Wales. He was treated as a naughty boy, who knew no better, and sent to prison for twelve days, a sentence which was extended to a month. Penry had gone to prison an innocent but left it, wary and determined in future to watch his every step; one fact he had learned was that the Court of High Commission was able to act quite independently of Parliament, to whom Penry had addressed his book.

He at once returned to the attack by writing a second and much more important treatise, which he called his Exhortation to the Governors and People of Wales. Once again he stressed the unhappy state of his country, emphasising his belief that the lawless behaviour of many Welshmen could only be changed if adequate religious teaching became available. He specifically criticised the Church of England in Wales for not preaching the

Gospel properly, above all condemning the Welsh bishops and suggesting that Welshmen should take it upon themselves to choose their own ministers. This indeed was fighting talk; with the censuring of the bishops the gauntlet had been thrown down, because to Elizabeth an attack on the bishops was tantamount to an attack on her authority, the bishops in her opinion providing a necessary balance between Church and State. This Exhortation was published by a travelling press, operating from secret locations, which government agents failed to find. This printing press, of which John Penry was probably the manager, produced a steady stream of Puritan pamphlets, of which this one alone took up the cudgels on behalf of Wales.

The year was 1588 and the Armada was soon to beat its way up the Channel; the Exhortation could hardly have appeared at a less opportune time. Nevertheless it was shortly after followed by another such publication, the Supplication, which was actually presented to Parliament. Its opening words were these. "Behold the mountains of Wales do now, in the thirty-first year of Queen Elizabeth's reign, call upon heaven and earth to witness that they are weary of the dumb ministers, the non-resident Lord Bishops etc. and they desire to be watered by the dew of Christ's Holy Gospel". Accompanying this treatise to Parliament was a note from the author, begging Parliament "to have poor Wales in remembrance". All was in vain and John Penry, who had by this time married Eleanor Godley, went into hiding, before long, deeming it wise to flee to Scotland, where for two years he stayed with friends, beyond the reach of the authority of England. In 1592 however he took the fatal decision to go back to London, where he attached himself to the Separatists, a Puritan sect, which was the spiritual father of Congregationalism.

Coinciding with this secret return of John Penry to London was the application of an act of Parliament, passed earlier in the year, designed "to punish persons obstinately refusing to come to church", an act intended to bring to book the Separatists, many of whose leaders were already in prison. Before long Penry was arrested at an open-air meeting of Separatists and quickly recognised as the author of the Exhortation; he was in consequence charged with being a seditious traitor, who endangered the security of the State and threatened the life of the Queen. On May 29th 1593, Penry was hanged; he was just thirty. Mourned by few beyond his wife and their four daughters, Deliverance, Comfort, Safety and Sure Hope, Penry's only aim had been to find ways and means of helping the poor and underprivileged, the wicked and the irreligious in his native Wales. The sad fact was however that in his short life no fellow Welshman worked with him in that field. He had been born half a century too soon; all the same let him be remembered and revered for giving his life for his friends.

B
Notes and Illustrations
Sequel to the Dissolution of the Monasteries

Earlier mention has been made of the ruinous state of most of the monasteries in the 1530s, when Thomas Cromwell, acting on the orders of his royal master, caused them to be suppressed. Of the monasteries in Wales Tintern alone had a full complement of monks. The fact however that most of these religious houses had for the most part outlived their usefulness, hardly gave the King the right to confiscate their property and to take away their lands. In 1539, by which time most of the forcible transfer of land and prosperity had taken place, Parliament stepped in and passed a law which legalised all these expropriations.

The subsequent history of three well-known Welsh religious houses, two Cistercian and one Augustinian, may be of interest to readers.

Tintern Abbey (*Abaty Tyndyrn*)

Tintern Abbey, especially if the sun is shining, seems an earthly paradise; in a sylvan setting on the banks of the river Wye, five miles upstream from Chepstow, stands this much-loved ruin, where William Wordsworth once listened to "the still sad music of humanity". In the twelfth century, however, when the first Cistercian monks came that way, they decided to settle and to build there because the site was so wild and so remote, and so isolated from the busy haunts of man, which Cistercians always avoided.

After the dissolution the abbey passed into the keeping of the Earl of Worcester, whose family retained possession of the ruins until the Crown moved in and bought Tintern from the family in 1901. In 1875, when the Worcester family still owned Tintern, Kilvert, the Victorian diarist, visited Tintern on a day trip in a coach from Chepstow; he seems to have been the only passenger who bothered to savour the beauty of the abbey ruins and the

PARTRISHOW

This church was visited in the 12th c. by Archbishop Baldwin and his faithful chaplain, Giraldus Cambrensis; from the steps of the churchyard cross, near the south door, Baldwin invited his audience to join the Third Crusade. Energetic historical enthusiasts may care, after admiring the wonderful screen in the church and studying the churchyard, to walk about a hundred yards down the hill, at the foot of which may still be seen a holy well, without which there would have been no church today.

Tradition has it that Issui, a 6th c. Christian missionary, who lived in a cell near this well, ministered to the neighbourhood, whose sick he had the power to heal until one day he was murdered. The same tradition insists that thereafter Issui's healing powers were transferred to the well itself, to which in the 11th c. a wealthy leper came and received a miraculous cure for his terrible affliction. Whereupon in gratitude he paid for a church to be built on top of the hill, a church which was dedicated to the Martyred Issui, which gradually became simplified into Partrishow, which in Welsh is called Patrisio.

monastic buildings. He "climbed to the top of the walls . . . adorned with a perfect wildflower garden of scarlet poppies, white roses, yellow stonecrop and purple mallow, which formed a low hedge along each side of the otherwise undefended footpath".

It is perhaps difficult today in Tintern to realise that an iron industry had flourished thereabouts since very early, probably Roman times, the plentiful supply of wood providing the means of smelting the locally-produced ore. The monks are thought to have organised successfully this manufacture of iron, which survived the dissolution and indeed prospered — in different hands of course — until about 1820. In addition a plaque outside the abbey draws the attention of visitors to the fact that it was in Tintern in 1568 that brass was first made by fusing together copper and zinc.

Strata Florida *(Ystrad Fflur)*

Strata Florida, the second Cistercian abbey to be visited, lies two miles north of Tregaron in Dyfed; its situation today, unlike that of Tintern, is nearly as remote and in winter nearly as bleak as it must have been in the twelfth century when it was founded. In its prime the monastery was very prosperous thanks to the wool trade which had greatly flourished in the expert hands of the monks and it became a centre of culture and influence.

At the dissolution the abbey and its precincts were given to the Stedman family, who retained it until the eighteenth century when the male line of the Stedmans died out. It then passed to the family of Richard Stedman's wife, the Powells, which in 1739 built a splendid mansion at Nanteos, two and a half miles south-east of Aberystwyth. When the Powells left Strata Florida and went to Nanteos, they took with them a certain artifact, which had been entrusted to the monks of Strata Florida shortly before the dissolution.

The story goes that Joseph of Arimathea, after the crucifixion of Christ, settled in Glastonbury, bringing with him the wooden cup from which Christ had drunk at the Last Supper. The tradition persisted and the monks of Glastonbury jealously guarded their precious secret until news of the impending dissolution of

TINTERN ABBEY
One of the six great Cistercian abbeys of Wales.

STRATA FLORIDA ABBEY
Visitors to this Cistercian abbey are recommended to round off their pilgrimage with a walk through the neighbouring churchyard, which surrounds the parish church; there under a huge yew tree may still be identified the grave of Dafydd ap Gwilym, Wales' foremost medieval poet. The tree is believed to have been planted on the grave by the monks of Strata Florida.

Glastonbury reached them, when several of their number carried it over the hills to Strata Florida for safe custody. When the Stedmans took over from the monks at Strata Florida, they promised to take care of this Holy Grail, two hundred years later handing it over to the Powells, who took it with them when they moved from Strata Florida to Nanteos. Gradually magic properties were assigned to the blackened piece of olive wood; indeed until the early years of the twentieth century the Powells allowed sick people in their neighbourhood to borrow the cup, on condition that on recovery, when they brought the cup back, they would sign a statement, confirming that they had been restored to health. The last known note is dated 1903. Thereafter presumably the cup stayed with the Powell family, but in 1967 they moved house, it is believed, to a new home in Herefordshire.

One final note: Strata Florida today, remotely situated as it is, possesses a modern and an admirably equipped museum on the site.

Llanthony Priory *(Llanddewi Nant Honddu)*

This Augustinian ruin is superbly situated in the Honddu Valley in Gwent, about six miles north of Llanfihangel Crucorney, on the main road from Abergavenny to Hereford. Visitors are recommended, while in this valley, also to make a small detour to see the little church at Cwmyoy, and, if possible also to savour the unique charm of Partrishow Church, in the next valley to the west, the Grwyne Fawr.

At the dissolution of Llanthony in 1538 the last prior received a small pension and the buildings and the surrounding land were sold by the King to the Chief Justice of Ireland, Nicholas Arnolde; in later years the estate was sold to the Harleys, who kept it until 1790, when it was bought by a Colonel Wood, from Brecon, who turned the Prior's lodgings into a comfortable house for himself and equipped the south tower of the West front as a shooting lodge for his sporting guests.

The history of Llanthony changed direction in 1807, when the new owner was none other than the celebrated poet Walter Savage Landor, he who, on his seventy-fifth birthday, referred to "warming both hands before the fire of life". In 1807 this friend of Browning and Swinburne paid £20,000 for his estate, which he fondly intended to transform into something unusually splendid. Landor's gifts, however, were poetic rather than practical and in addition he never succeeded in acquiring any understanding of his neighbours in the Honddu valley, or indeed in making any agreement with them. Hence his elaborate schemes all came to nothing and he decamped to Italy, leaving the estate with his mother, who organised it so well that the Landor family still lived there in 1870, when Kilvert (who else?!) paid it two visits.

On the first occasion, early in April the diarist was sorely put out by having to wait, while two tourists, who had had the temerity to order dinner before him, finished a leisurely meal. Kilvert, keen readers will have noticed, disliked tourists even more than he did dissenters! The entry in the diary for Tuesday, April 5th, 1870 is well worth reading as is the account of his subsequent visit two months later on Midsummer Day, when his arrival coincided with Mrs Landor's Rent Day, when all her tenants were being entertained by her to dinner. In the unusual circumstances Kilvert and his party had to make do, we are told, with only bread, butter, cheese, beer and boiled eggs (of which they consumed twenty!)

Llanthony today is in the best possible hands, those of the Department of the Environment; the ruins are, of course, well cared for and the Archaeological Department of the University of Cardiff have been allowed every summer since 1978 to carry out scientific digging. Much new and valuable information has been discovered about this medieval priory, and undoubtedly future digs there will yield up many more archaeological secrets.

Meanwhile, Col. Wood's house is now a comfortable hotel, whose guests have to find their way to their beds up a spiral staircase, while in the cellar which is part of the medieval undercroft, real ale may be obtained, thus making possible a return to the hospitality enjoyed by visitors to the religious houses of the Middle Ages.

LLANTHONY PRIORY

Four miles higher up the Honddu valley above Llanthony Priory is
Capel-y-ffin, where the confusingly-named Llanthony Monastery was
established in 1869 by an eccentric English monk, Father Ignatius. Readers
are referred to Kilvert's diaries for several contemporary accounts of the
short-lived monastery and its remarkable founder, who claimed to have been
visited several times by visions of the Holy Virgin at Capel-y-ffin. The Rev.
Joseph Leycester Lyne, alias Father Ignatius, who died in 1908, lies buried in
the ruins of his monastery, his grave marked by a cross of stones.

Gruffydd Robert in Exile

In the middle of the 16th century this most illustrious of Welsh Roman Catholic scholars languished for twenty years in Milan, from where he wrote nostalgically . . . " . . . although fair the place where we are now, yet I long for many things which were to be had in Wales . . . if you wanted entertainment, you could find a minstrel and his harp to play gentle airs or a singer of sweet ditties to sing to the harp . . . if you wished to hear about the customs of the country, there would be gray-haired old men who would relate every remarkable and worthy deed in the land of Wales since time immemorial . . . as for the vineyards here, although they look beautiful enough, yet a Welshman's heart does not respond to them, as it would to the banks of the Dee or the Vale of Clwyd, or in many other places I could name from St David's to Holyhead . . . my heart would gladden sooner to hear the cuckoo sing in my own country than it would here on hearing the sweet notes of the nightingale . . . "

(from *A Book of Wales*, by Meic Stephens, published by J.M. Dent 1987).

Pilgrimage to Tŷ Mawr

For those who like to see their history on the ground as well as to read it in their armchairs, an excursion from Penmachno is suggested; little persuasion should be necessary to make attractive a country walk from there to Tŷ Mawr in the Wybrnant Valley. Tŷ Mawr may be approached, it is true, by a number of paths from the Lledr Valley but the walk from Penmachno is recommended because there is a meaningful Christian connection between the two places.

There was a time when pilgrimages were popular pursuits (Chaucer's *Canterbury Tales* will spring to readers' minds); in very early Christian times the most popular goal was Rome, where Peter and Paul died, but Rome, of course, was beyond the reach of most would-be pilgrims. The earliest such pilgrimage in Wales, it seems, was to Bardsey Island, which over the years found such favour with the church authorities that three pilgrimages to

WILLIAM MORGAN

The future bishop was born at Ty Mawr, where his father was a tenant of Sir John Wynn; his translation of the Bible first appeared in 1588, the year when the Armada came up the Channel.

TY MAWR

Birthplace of Bishop Morgan, now a National Trust property.

Bardsey were regarded as equal to one to Rome! Recalling this tradition, another Christian pilgrimage is here suggested, on foot, of course, from Penmachno to Tŷ Mawr, a Christian journey that spans a thousand years of history. First of all to get to Penmachno, take the A5 westwards from Pentrefoelas; after about seven miles turn left on to the B4406, which, after a further three miles, leads to Penmachno, a large village, where a car may be left. The church is locked, but a notice in the porch indicates a nearby house where the key may be obtained. In this church will be found four inscribed memorial stones, all taken from Romano-British graves in the neighbourhood, all dating from the fifth to the early sixth centuries. With one in particular of these stones pilgrims will be especially concerned; first however it has to be stressed that Wales is singularly fortunate in possessing a great many of these early Christian memorial stones, which commemorate the lives of Christians, who died long before Augustine brought Christianity to Kent in the late sixth century. Of all these early stones, two only in the whole of Wales bear the exciting Chi-Rho monogram, which is a joining-together of the first two Greek letters in Christ's name (see the illustration); one of these Chi-Rho stones is here in Penmachno church, its Latin inscription indicating that "Carausius lies here in this heap of stones".

With an Ordnance Survey map as an essential companion, now take the western road out of the village and after less than a mile follow the path through the woods to the right of the road, which, after two more miles of forest trails, leads down to Tŷ Mawr, the farm-house, where William Morgan was born. This one-time farm is now a museum belonging to the National Trust and, in Jan Morris' appropriate words, a national shrine; it is in the safe custody of the National Trust. Morgan's Welsh Bible, published in 1588, did as much for Wales as the Royal Navy's defeat of the Spanish Armada in the same year did for England.

Sir John Wynn

John Wynn (1553-1626) of Gwydir in the Conwy Valley, succeeded to the extensive Gwydir estates in 1580, thereafter devoting much

SIR JOHN WYNN

An ambitious, strong-minded landowner in the Conwy valley, as well as seeking the advancement of his family estates, he devoted much time and mental energy to improving the economic state of north Wales. It has already been told how he had hoped, though in vain, to have the Traeth Mawr, near Porthmadog reclaimed from the sea; in addition he managed his lead mines and had firm plans, which failed to come to fruition, for developing the copper resources of Anglesey and for setting up a clothing workshop in the Conwy valley, where he was quite prepared to bring weavers over from Ireland to provide the necessary man power.

GWYDIR CASTLE

Situated on the west bank of the Conwy river, across from Llanrwst, Gwydir Castle was first started in the 15th century, but enlarged and mostly rebuilt in the early years of the 16th century by Sir John Wynn, in whose opinion the castle became "the finest house in all north Wales". It survived more or less intact until the 19th century, when most of it was pulled down, and what survived this demolition was consumed in a great fire in the 1920s. The present extensive house, adorned by many a peacock, is almost entirely a 20th century reconstruction.

of his time to adding to the prosperity and affluence of his family, with the result that the Wynns became the most powerful family in North Wales. After several terms of office as Sheriff, both of Caernarfonshire and of Meirionnydd, he became the member of Parliament for Caernarfon; in 1606 he was knighted by James I, who three years later made him a baronet.

Posterity however remembers him above all for the fact that he wrote the history of his family, in which an invaluable picture is painted of the social history of North Wales at that time. This *History of the Gwydir Family* is an important piece of contemporary Welsh history, which is now available in an English translation, which the Gomer Press published in 1990.

An indication of the historical value of this family history and its attendant Memoirs is provided by an idea Sir John Wynn entertained for the possible reclamation of land in Traeth Mawr, near the modern Porthmadog, which was a part of the Gwydir estates. Readers will find later in this book an account of the eventual successful reclamation of Traeth Mawr at the beginning of the nineteenth century by William Madocks. However a letter survives in which Sir John Wynn invited Sir Hugh Middleton to take an interest in draining Traeth Mawr, Sir Hugh having recently been successful in winning back from the sea some two thousand acres in the Isle of Wight.

In this letter to his fellow baronet Sir John Wynn wrote:

" . . . My skill is little, my experience none at all in such matters . . . yet I ever had a desire to further my country in such actions as might be for their profit, and leave a remembrance of my endeavours . . . now seeing it pleased God to bring you into this country, I am to desire you to take a view of the place, not being above a day's journey from you; and if you do see things fit to be undertaken, I am content to adventure a brace of hundred pounds to join you in the work".

Sir John died a few months later.

In Retrospect

Looking back over four hundred years and more to the sixteenth century, it can be seen that Wales in that century had been annexed by England, that Welsh people in their public affairs had been prevented from using their own language, and had also had a change of religion foisted upon them. Yet in 1586, when Camden's *Britannia* was published, he could write:

> "Mary, Elizabeth and Edward, the children of Henry VIII, although they received not the investiture, yet styled themselves Princes of Wales. For at that time Wales was by the Act of Union so united and incorporated into England that they enjoyed the same laws and privileges".

No matter how superficial that judgement, nevertheless it was true that most Welsh people had come to accept the Act of Union, failing as yet to realise the long-term significance of the banning of the Welsh language from their courts of law. It seems also to be true that by the end of this sixteenth century Wales had, generally speaking, accepted the Reformation. This more or less tacit acceptance by the Welsh of what was an English Reformation arose partly through the general Welsh ignorance of English, which naturally tended to result in Welsh indifference, and partly because the English-trained priests provided the main channel of communication for English ideas to pass into Wales. This continuing stream of English influence through a church system, which was based on Canterbury, was, happily for those Welshmen, who could see the dangerous drift of events, to be splendidly offset by the ever-increasing use in the seventeenth century of the Welsh Book of Common Prayer and of William Morgan's Welsh Bible, which succeeded in preserving for posterity the widespread use of the Welsh language, and with it the means of maintaining an essentially different culture.

A
Part II The Seventeenth Century Upheaval

a. The Outlook in the New Century

Just a hundred years before, many Welshmen will have greeted the new century with some optimism; their country was not yet a part of England but fifteen years previously a Welshman, Henry Tudor, having beaten and killed the King of England in battle at Bosworth, had made himself King. Bosworth was regarded in Wales as a great away victory! For, a long and bitter quarrel with England had ended, as they saw it, in a great and glorious victory. Henry VII however did very little to alter the government of Wales; the six counties of Anglesey (*Môn*), Caernarfon, Meirionnydd, Flint, Cardigan (*Ceredigion*) and Carmarthen (*Caerfyrddin*) had since the reign of Edward I been directly ruled from London, but the Marches after 1485 were governed by the newly-revived Council of Marches, based on Ludlow, which acted as a bridge between central authority in London and the people of the Marches. In addition, Henry VII sensibly placed in key positions in Wales Welsh leaders like Sir Rhys ap Thomas, who had won his knighthood on the field of Bosworth.

After 1536, when Parliament passed the Act of Union, which finally made Wales politically a part of England, English ideas spread more rapidly in Wales, one of which was beginning to have considerable social and political consequence. In the Middle Ages the Welsh law of inheritance was known as gavelkind, whereby at a man's death his property was equally divided up between his sons; this traditional way of doing things, which had begun to be ignored by some in the fourteenth century, disintegrated very quickly in the sixteenth, when it was wholly replaced by the rule of inheritance in favour east of Offa's Dyke, that of primogeniture, whereby the eldest son inherited all his late father's estate. Hence in the sixteenth century there grew up in Wales a new rural middle class, whose power was based on land. These 'new' men developed a strong vested interest in the success of the Tudor dynasty, which they served by officiating at the Petty Sessions: moreover they sent their sons to be educated at English universities, in order to prepare them eventually to follow in their father's footsteps.

Early on in the new century, in 1603, Elizabeth died, and with her ended the Welsh dynasty of the Tudors; with the succession of James I to the throne, there began a new dynasty, that of the Scottish Stuarts, a change which may well have caused many Welshmen to anticipate the future with some apprehension. The acid test was thought likely to be the way the new King treated the Council of the Marches, which in fact was to continue to exist in Ludlow for another forty years. Over the years influential and ambitious Welshmen, leaders of the new middle class, had tended to foregather at Ludlow, where they sought to engage the ear of every Englishman, who happened to be the Lord President. Power may have ebbed from Ludlow, but influence continued to flow. James I, not always the wisest of men, on this occasion displayed shrewdness in his treatment of influential Welshmen, who, thus encouraged, transferred their previous allegiance to the old Tudors to the new Stuarts.

The history of the seventeenth century (and it is the history of Wales as well as of England), was bedevilled by the great quarrel between the King and his Parliament; thanks to the perspective which the intervening passage of three hundred years and more allows, it is possible to see the development of this contest, like the plot of a great drama unfolding itself. Pressure built up quite early in the century in the reign of James I, leading to the call to arms in mid-century and, as the tumultuous century was drawing to its close, a momentous dénouement held the stage in the settlement of 1688.

The quarrel between King and Parliament, which forty years later was to lead to a bitter civil war had its beginning in the reign of James I; its causes were manifold, of which two in particular need here to be stressed. Firstly, the prevalent political doctrine at this time in Europe was a belief in the divinity of kings, a view passionately held by James I. Parliament on the other hand, despite occasional periods of abject subservience to Tudor rulers, gradually but surely, as its members were more and more drawn from the merchant middle class, refused to believe that any king of England could interpret the will of God and, in so doing, stood up increasingly for the rights of the King's subjects. This fundamental difference of opinion between King and Parliament first assumed serious proportions in the closing years of James I's reign, when a second cause of dissension arose, which concerned the amount of money Parliament was prepared to give to the King.

In those far-off days financial responsibility for the carrying-on of government, whether it was for the waging of wars or of paying servants of the Crown, from all-powerful diplomats to common soldiers, alike rested on the shoulders of the monarch, who, in turn, of course, depended upon Parliament once a year to vote him the necessary money. James I soon came to realise that his predecessor on the throne, Elizabeth had left the royal exchequer sparsely furnished — the war with Spain had seen to that! Parliament for its part was perhaps less than understanding of the royal predicament, which became worse during James' reign, as the value of our currency dropped. Europe at the beginning of the seventeenth century was indeed suffering from a very modern economic disease, inflation, which had been made very much worse by the large quantity of silver, brought back to Europe by the Spaniards from their conquests in central America. Parliament however ignored, as parliaments sometimes do, basic economic facts, and refused to make an adequate increase in their contribution to the royal exchequer; hence James had to look around for alternative methods of raising money. This, in general terms, was the background against which the great drama of the seventeenth century was played out, a drama in which a Welshman, a product of the new rural middle class previously referred to, was to play a leading part.

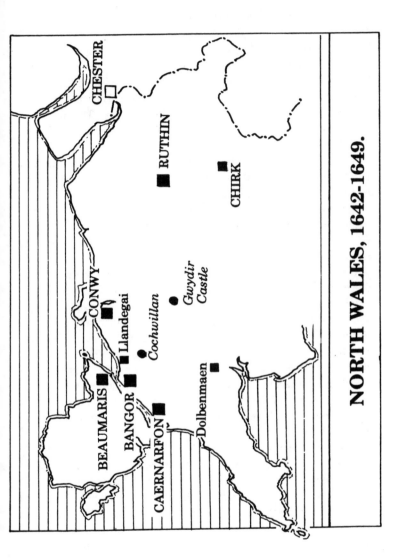

NORTH WALES, 1642-1649.

CHESTER

RUTHIN

CHIRK

CONWY
Llandegai
Cochwillan
Gwydir Castle

BEAUMARIS

BANGOR

CAERNARFON
Dolbenmaen

47

b. A Welshman in High Places

John Williams was born in 1582 in Conwy, the second son of Edward and Mary Williams, his illustrious godfather being Sir John Wynn. On his father's side he was descended from a younger branch of the Gruffydd family of Penrhyn; their fifteenth century home at Cochwillan, east of the A5 between Llandygái and Bethesda has miraculously managed to survive. His mother's forebears were none other than the Wynns, whose mansion at Gwydir near Llanrwst in the Conwy Valley was likewise built in the fifteenth century. All his life John Williams regarded himself first and foremost as a son of Conwy, within whose historic walls many momentous events in his later life took place.

He was educated at Ruthin Grammar School before in 1598 going up to Cambridge, where on his own admission he knew more Greek and Latin than he did English, causing him to be the friendly butt of his fellow students for his Welsh turn of speech. After graduating in theology at Cambridge, John Williams was ordained and prepared himself for a successful career in the church, to which his qualifications, his background and his affluence clearly pointed. Meanwhile storm clouds were gathering in the world outside, as the conflict started to take shape between the King and his Parliament, between those who favoured a despotic monarchy and those who preferred sovereignty to reside to Parliament. As the struggle loomed nearer, James came to rely more and more on the advice of extra-parliamentary noblemen, of whom by far the most influential was the future Duke of Buckingham, who was in time also to become the close friend and confidant of Charles I.

In 1611, John Williams was invited to preach before James I and so impressed his royal audience that thereafter not only did his career take off in a spectacular fashion but it also began to suggest political advancement too, especially when in 1612 the Lord Chancellor, Lord Ellesmere, the most powerful politician in the land, made him his chaplain. Soon the King himself was asking Williams his opinions on matters of state. Religious preferment followed in 1619, with his appointment as Dean of Salisbury, and again in 1620 when Williams became Dean of Westminster, an appointment as lucrative as it was prestigious. The widespread belief that he was developing political ambitions received astonishing confirmation in 1621, when in addition to becoming Bishop of Lincoln, he was also appointed Lord Keeper of the Seal. Thus before his thirty-ninth birthday John Williams, despite being a bishop, was already even higher up the political ladder.

The rocket that had ascended so brilliantly into the political sky, began to fall back in the last years of James' reign, only to crash to earth soon after Charles succeeded his father in 1625. Within the first months of the new reign twice the King sought Williams' opinion and twice he counselled moderation, and twice had his counsel ignored. From that time Charles grew to depend more and more on the Duke of Buckingham and a new rising star in the Church of England, William Laud, who like the Duke, was a strong believer in the divine right of kings. Before 1625 had ended John Williams had been dismissed from his high office of state. He then retired, for the time being, to his see at Lincoln, where for the next twelve years, until 1637, he lived in the grand manner, entertaining munificently. These were years of immense importance, and although he was of necessity an enforced spectator of national events, he was by no means unaware or unmoved by them.

Crisis followed crisis as the King was forced by his desperate need for money to summon Parliament, only to dismiss it, when Members tried to put a brake on royal autocracy. The King, such was his dire need, tried again but Parliament, in whose ranks were numbered men of the calibre of John Hampden and his cousin, Oliver Cromwell, before taking any decision about what money to vote to the royal exchequer, pushed through the Commons in 1628 the Petition of Right; this Act, one of the great charters of our liberties, made illegal any royal demand for money, unless sanctioned by Parliament and in addition forbade the imprisonment of any citizen without due cause being given. John Williams, staunch supporter of monarchy though he was, wrote urgently to the King from Lincoln, begging him to accept this Petition of Right, but the King thought otherwise, dismissed Parliament and from 1629-1640 ruled the country without once summoning Parliament.

In these long years of arbitrary royal rule the position of William Laud became ever stronger; sensing the rivalry to be expected from John Williams, Laud carefully gathered evidence of what he regarded as Williams' illegal actions over the years, alleging betrayal of state secrets and perjury. Laud's hand was much strengthened in 1633 when Charles made him Archbishop of Canterbury. Finally his dossier on John Williams complete, Laud had him arrested, his fellow-bishop be it remembered, and hauled him up before the infamous Court of Star Chamber in London, where various charges were brought against him. The outcome was that Williams was fined £10,000, suspended from the deanery of Westminster and from the bishopric of Lincoln, and packed off to the Tower of London, where he was to stay until 1640.

Any relief that Laud may have felt after the imprisonment of his rival must have been short-lived because John Williams was to prove as unpleasant a thorn in his side in prison as he had been outside, with the result that in 1639 he was taken from the Tower to face the Court of Star Chamber once again, this time on a charge of libelling the Archbishop of Canterbury. Again Williams was heavily fined before being returned to the Tower of London. Late in the following year, 1640, the King, reduced to desperately straitened circumstances by lack of money which he required to finance a war against the Scots, had to swallow his pride and summon Parliament. At once this Parliament released John Williams from prison; this was the Long Parliament whose objective was to get the legal relationship of the King to Parliament clearly defined and for ever enshrined in statute. To make their task the easier, they first ordered the arrest of Laud; the King, thus bereft of his normal source of support, decided, in an attempt to win over public opinion, to summon John Williams to advise him once more. By the end of 1641 his fortunes seemed about to be restored to their former height, when the King made him

Archbishop of York. By this preferment Williams was now virtually Head of the Church of England, as Laud was never to leave the Tower, except to be executed in 1645.

Meanwhile great events were being set in train; Parliament, under the leadership of John Pym drew up the Grand Remonstrance, which was then debated at great length and with rising passions. It amounted to a vote of No Confidence in the King, which, when put to the vote, was only carried by a meagre majority of eleven. The King, who was much encouraged by the unexpected strength of the parliamentary opposition to Pym, decided on action. On January 5th, 1642, Charles went down to Westminster and attempted to arrest the ring-leaders, including Pym himself. The Five Members, notified in advance of what was afoot, had made good their escape. This abortive and illegal act on the King's part was the last meeting of King and Parliament before the recourse to arms. After this humiliating farce the King left London, to which he never returned, of his own free will. John Williams, in June 1642, went to York to be consecrated Archbishop. Two months later the Royal Standard was raised in Nottingham and the Civil War had begun. When John Williams learned that a party of parliamentary soldiers was approaching his palace, he fled from York and sought the security of the walls of Conwy Castle.

At this climacteric in John Williams' career it is salutary to pause a moment and take stock; he had already achieved the highest positions in two different spheres, in church and state. To have kept the Great Seal of England and to have become the virtual Head of the Church of England was a remarkable feat indeed, especially for a man who at the outset was a scholar with no obvious inclination for a career that would lead to political or spiritual pre-eminence. And now, in 1642, on the morrow of his consecration as an archbishop, John Williams, having already celebrated his sixtieth birthday, at a time when many men might have looked longingly forward to a life of slippered ease in a well-earned retirement, instead stood upon the threshold of a third career, that of a soldier in the service of his royal master.

c. The Impact of the Civil War

It is necessary at this stage of the unfolding drama to introduce a new character, whose path was to cross that of the archbishop for the next four years. This new character was John Owen, than whom North Wales produced no more unswervingly loyal supporter of the royal cause. After the lapse of more than three hundred years it should be possible today to view the clash between these two leaders of men dispassionately, while still registering dismay that such a clash ever took place. John Owen hailed from the remote and beautiful Pennant Valley, west of Snowdon, his family home, Clenennau, lying between Dolbenmaen and Penmorfa. His father had been secretary to Elizabeth's great man of mystery, Sir Francis Walsingham. John succeeded to the family estate in 1626, becoming Sheriff of Caernarfon four years later, when he was only thirty years of age.

An up and coming man, he also became Sheriff of Merioneth the following year. In the very prime of life, when the Civil War broke out in 1642, John Owen was at once commissioned by the King to raise and train an army in the counties of Gwynedd, Anglesey, Meirionnydd and Caernarfon.

It was in that same year that John Williams returned to Conwy from York; after a brief visit to Oxford, where he pledged his loyalty to the King, Williams went back to Conwy, where he attended to the needs of the town and castle. At his own expense he greatly improved the fortifications of the castle, he laid in supplies and he strengthened the garrison. Meanwhile he kept in constant touch with the King, being Charles' chief and most valuable source of information on developments in North Wales and more particularly in Ireland, where a full-blooded rebellion had broken out in 1641. Ormonde had been despatched there by the King to try to contain the outbreak, taking with him an army, in the ranks of which were many Welshmen. By 1643 the Irish rebellion seemed to have quitened down sufficiently for Ormonde to agree to the King's request to send home the Welsh contingent. John Williams made detailed arrangements for the eventual reception of the

Welsh soldiers both in Beaumaris and in Conwy, where the returning soldier were to be fed, reclothed and rearmed for further service in the royal cause nearer home. By the end of 1643, John Williams was ready for anything; he still awaited the arrival of the Welsh soldiers, whose return in fact Ormonde was never to authorise. At any rate Conwy Castle was equipped for all eventualities, prompting Williams before the year was out to ask his royal master to make him its Governor.

John Owen, meanwhile, having duly raised and armed an army in Gwynedd, as the King had ordered, marched at its head into England; he took part in an engagement outside Oxford in May 1643, then in July he commanded a brigade under Prince Rupert at the siege of Bristol, where he was wounded, recovering in time to participate in further fighting at Newbury in September. It was not until April 1946 that Owen was back in Caernarfon, where the King promptly made him Sheriff again. From that moment John Williams had a rival on the spot; in December of the same year Williams learned to his chagrin that the Governorship of Conwy to which he had aspired had been given to John Owen, along with a knighthood. Spurned as he felt himself to have been, John Williams stayed on in Conwy Castle as the 'de facto' Governor until Sir John Owen forcibly but legally expelled the archbishop, who for the time being withdrew to Bangor.

This local quarrel, humiliating as it was for John Williams, was of little consequence compared with the grave decline in the royalist fortunes not many miles away at Chester, to which important base a parliamentary army laid siege in the early summer of 1645. Throughout this fatal year for the King's cause Charles pleaded all in vain for reinforcements to be sent from Ireland; in a forlorn attempt to relieve the siege, Charles led an army against the parliamentary forces that were encamped outside the city walls. The resulting battle at Rowton Moor in September was disastrous for the King. Chester was to hold out for a few more months but finally surrendered to Parliament in May 1646.

After the fall of Chester the first Civil War virtually came to an end because Charles, feeling at the end of his tether, when his own headquarters at Oxford were shortly afterwards besieged, managed to slip out and surrendered to the Scottish army, which by that time had come as far south as Newark — the Scots were the allies of Parliament. John Williams, faced with a new situation after Chester's fall, wrote tactfully to Sir John Owen, hoping that thereby the breach between them might be narrowed but receiving only a dusty answer, made contact with Mytton, the Parliamentary general, who was in the process of systematically reducing those coastal towns in North Wales that had stood up for the King. It is interesting in this connection to discover that Williams' letter to Mytton drew a reply from none other than Oliver Cromwell, (who had been baptised Williams); in his letter Cromwell acknowledged himself to be the archbishop's cousin.

In the autumn Mytton's forces, now unexpectedly aided and abetted by Williams and his men, captured Conwy town and in November the castle itself, its defender Sir John Owen being allowed to leave and return to his home in the Pennant Valley, on certain stringent conditions. John Williams' defection, however, was no isolated affair as many of the gentry in North Wales, feeling that the war had been lost and that ordinary men and women in North Wales had suffered enough, also decided to throw in their lot with the parliamentary forces and so help to bring to a speedy conclusion a sorry chapter in the history of North Wales. Sir John, it must be said, stayed loyal to the King's cause, and somehow managed to escape from a death sentence passed on him in the aftermath. Indeed he lived long enough to welcome the restoration of the monarchy in 1660.

After the parliamentary capture of Conwy in 1646, John Williams went to live at Gloddaeth Hall, which still stands across the water from Conwy a mile or two behind Deganwy. There he spent his few remaining years, though it was, while he was staying with his kinsmen in Gwydir Castle, that he heard the news of Charles' execution in 1649, news which, some believe, caused him to regret his defection. In March 1650, John Williams died at Gloddaeth and was buried at Llandygái, where a monument on the church wall commemorates him, along with his helmet and spurs.

A scholar, a statesman, a church leader and in his old age a man of action, John Williams was a true son of the Renaissance and one of the greatest Welshmen of his age; in a quieter century he would have been able to devote more of his time to his undoubted love of fine arts, music and architecture. The archbishop was certainly an opportunist but also a man of wise moderation, whose counsels, had they been heeded, might well have guided the storm-tossed ship of state into calmer waters.

Summing up the course of the Civil War in Wales, in the early days in general most people were on the King's side, parliamentary support being restricted to south Pembrokeshire and the areas around Chirk and Ruthin where Sir Thomas Myddleton had his way. In addition to the Welsh gentry and the middle class, who had derived most benefit from the Act of Union, there was also a very considerable contingent of Welsh regular soldiers fighting for the King.

d. Wales Under the Commonwealth

When Charles I was executed in 1649, the government of England was firmly in the hands of the sixty survivors of the original Long Parliament, known as the Rump. Theirs was the difficult task of ruling Wales, their agents Oliver Cromwell and the Army, whose object was to encourage the spread of Puritanism there. Today Wales is thought of as being more nonconformist than England, and certainly there is a proliferation of nonconformist chapels up and down the country. At the end of the Civil War however the Puritan Movement, which in England had provided Oliver Cromwell with such sturdy support, had hardly touched Wales. Evidence of early scattered nonconformist activity was to be found in Wrexham, which became a Puritan stronghold through Walter Cradoc and Morgan Llwyd, in Radnorshire, where the Baptist voices of Hugh Evans and Vavasor Powell were raised aloft, in the Gower Peninsula where the first Baptist chapel in Wales was established by John Miles in 1649, and in Gwent, at Llanfaches, north of Newport, where an independent chapel had been

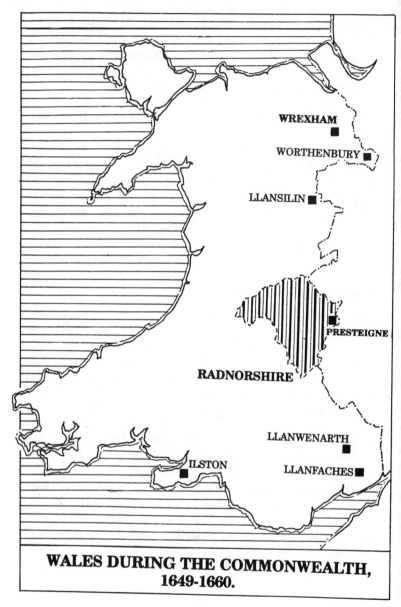

WREXHAM ■

WORTHENBURY ■

LLANSILIN ■

PRESTEIGNE ■

RADNORSHIRE

LLANWENARTH ■

ILSTON ■

LLANFACHES ■

**WALES DURING THE COMMONWEALTH,
1649-1660.**

consecrated in 1639 by the former vicar, who had been driven out for his "Puritanical leanings". Apart from these rather isolated exceptions there was little enough Puritanism to encourage Cromwell, who early on in the Commonwealth settled some of his time-expired soldiers in Radnorshire, in the hope that they might be successful evangelists. The Rump Parliament, alerted to the extent of the problem by Cromwell, in 1650 passed an Act for the Better Propagation of the Gospel in Wales.

A God-fearing cavalry officer, Colonel Thomas Harrison was named by Parliament to see that the provisions of the Act were duly carried out; under him were appointed seventy commissioners, with Col. John Jones put in charge of North Wales and Col. Philip Jones in charge of the South. Their task was in the course of the following three years to seek out and to expel unsatisfactory priests and teachers; by 1653, when their work had to end and the Act lapsed, three hundred priests and teachers had lost their jobs. This sort of arbitrary action, however conscientiously carried out by soldiers, could hardly fail to produce dissatisfaction and with it quite unsatisfactory results. And so it proved, especially as it gave rise to a new and intractable problem, namely how to find adequate replacements for those who had been driven out.

In an attempt to solve this problem a system was established whereby a panel of itinerant preachers was enrolled to whom districts were assigned in which they were to preach and teach; such an arrangement could hardly have succeeded, had all the chosen preachers been educated men, but as in many cases zeal ssemed their only obvious qualification, some of the consequences were lamentable. Nevertheless among the chosen were some outstanding men, men of the calibre of Morgan Llwyd, who had originally gone to Wrexham to learn at the feet of Walter Cradoc; in the Civil War he had fought for Parliament, but thereafter he devoted his life to preaching and writing, and during the "itinerant preaching experiment" had been responsible for a very large area which included a part of Caernarfonshire.

Another of these preachers was Hugh Evans, a Radnorshire Baptist, who, before being enrolled for itinerant preaching had

RADNORSHIRE IN THE 17TH CENTURY.

Newtown

Llanidloes

BEGUILDY

KNUCKLAS

KNIGHTON

R. Teme

R. Wye

RHAEADR

NANTMEL

The Pales

PRESTEIGNE

NEW RADNOR

DISSERTH

GLASCWM

Builth Wells

PAINSCASTLE

Maes-yr-onnen

Hay

R. Wye

10 8 6 4 2 0   10 ML.
10 8 6 4 2 0   10 KM.

been successful in making a Baptist connection in Radnorshire. In the same county lived Vavasor Powell, who was probably the best-known and most successful of the itinerant preachers. Radnorshire-born, he had been educated at Oxford; he first became a teacher before feeling the urge to preach. On one occasion, as a young man he had to appear at the Radnorshire Assizes in Presteigne in order to answer a charge of "disturbing the peace through preaching"! He too had supported Parliament in the Civil War, when he took every opportunity to exercise his power of preaching. Such was the reputation he gained as a public speaker, that in 1650 he was ordered to preach before Parliament in London. His subsequent contribution to itinerant preaching was substantial and successful, although, as will be seen later, his enemies remembered his achievements in after years.

However, Cromwell in 1653, discouraged by what seemed to him the failure of the itinerant preachers to supply the needs of Wales and disenchanted with the activities of the Rump, dismissed Parliament; this was the famous occasion, when the Mace was removed, along with all remaining traces of constitutional action. Oliver Cromwell's impatient dismissal of the Rump Parliament found favour with some extreme Puritans, especially with the sect, known as the Fifth Monarchists, who had some enthusiastic members in Wales; these people expected Christ to return to earth in the near future in order to rule here for a thousand years. Such Puritans became even more whole-hearted in their support for Cromwell, when later that same year, 1653, he indulged in another constitutional experiment by appointing a Parliament of a hundred and forty upright and God-fearing men (the six representatives chosen to speak for Wales were all selected by Vavasor Powell). This strange Government, the Rule of the Saints, sometimes known as the Barebones Parliament after the unusual name of one of its members, spent five months in eager, ineffectual chatter before being driven out by Cromwell, to the utter chagrin of extreme Puritans, whose friendly feelings towards Cromwell soon gave way to implacable hatred.

After several more unavailing experiments in government, one of which gave him the welcome title of the Lord Protector, Cromwell chose a simple solution, Army rule. The whole country was divided up into ten areas, over each of which presided a Major General, who had at his disposal units of the army to see that his decisions were carried out. Thus England passed under complete and open Army rule, which became, not surprisingly, everywhere thoroughly detested. These rigorous years of arbitrary military government did much to prepare the mind of the people for an eventual return to monarchy. Cromwell died in 1658, his son Richard briefly inheriting responsibility for governing the country. He soon called a parliament, which he quickly dismissed before himself resigning.

In 1659 the Rump was recalled; its first act was to abolish the Protectorate. In 1660 it invited the eldest son of the late Charles I to become King, and in May Charles II rode into London, to the joy and relief of the populace. It has too to be said that the news was received with widespread pleasure in Wales, where Charles was proclaimed King at Wrexham. Nevertheless it needs also to be clearly stated that, although noncomformity had as yet made little headway in Wales, such successful beginnings as had been made here and there in the country by Independents (Congregationalists), Baptists and Quakers were to assume great importance and give much needed hope in the dark days of intolerance that were to follow so soon on the restoration of the monarchy. Indication of the wrath to come was provided by the fates of Vavasor Powell, who had to languish in prison from 1661-7, and of Colonel John Jones, one of the commissioners appointed by Parliament in 1650 to weed out unsuitable Welsh priests, who was executed, while John Miles, who had built the first Baptist chapel in Wales at Ilston in the Gower, emigrated with most of his congregation to America.

e. The Spread of Nonconformity

Many were the flags of welcome, put out for the new King, in 1660 in Wales, where the Restoration rewarded successful and orthodox Welshmen, many of whom by this time, having become thoroughly anglicised, had been suitably promoted to posts of high responsibility in church and state. There was however a minority of Welshmen, who felt no particular wish to cheer or to share in the general jubilation. These odd men out were the nonconformists, who had become intoxicated by the heady wine of freedom, especially in the early 1650s. These simple people, some of whom, of course, may have been too simplistic, had seen a chance in the brave new world of the Commonwealth, to produce a new society, based on the underlying principles of the New Testament. The persecution that later accompanied the implementation of the new, reactionary anti-Puritan laws of the 1660s, after the dream had faded, seems in retrospect to have benefited the Quaker Movement most, because these remarkable people actually seem to have succeeded in thriving on persecution, as will be shown later.

First readers may like to be reminded how the Restoration Parliament reacted to the spread of the free religious thinking of the previous decade. From 1661 to 1665 four Acts of Parliament together clearly stated this new position; every member of a municipal council was required to take Holy Communion in his parish church (Corporation Act 1661). Every priest had to swear on oath of allegiance to the Book of Common Prayer and the Thirty Nine Articles, which had been accepted as the embodiment of the Anglican faith (Act of Uniformity 1662); two thousand clergymen forfeited their livings rather than take the oath. Any people attending a religious meeting of more than four persons, excluding members of a family, were liable to be sent to prison (Conventicle Act 1664; this was the act which put John Bunyan in Bedford Jail, thus giving him the opportunity to write The Pilgrim's Progress). Finally the Five Mile Act 1665 forbade any former priest, who had not taken the required oath, to live within five miles of a town or of his former church. The combined object of all these pieces of legislation was to destroy Puritanism; in the event these laws, though certainly reducing the number of religious dissidents, greatly strengthened the moral fibre of those who could not be forced to toe the line.

This firm sequence of repressive anti-dissident acts of Parliament was surprisingly — and only temporarily —

interrupted in 1672 by a Declaration of Indulgence made by Charles II (to the vexation of Parliament), whereby Christian worshippers, who were not members of the Church of England, would be allowed to hold services in private houses, provided that these houses were officially licensed for that purpose. Curious readers will have to be satisfied with the brief comment that such tolerance would benefit Roman Catholics as well as Non-conformists, and, at that particular moment Charles II had good reasons for wanting to favour Roman Catholics! As far as Wales was concerned, more than a few private houses were duly registered including, to take examples from only a single county, Radnorshire, a Baptist house in Llandrindod, an Independent one in New Radnor and a Presbyterian house in Beguildy.

This strange politically-inspired intermission of tolerance was of short duration, persecution soon resuming its former course against nonconformists, until in 1688 the second great revolution of the seventeenth century took place. This so-called Glorious Revolution (glorious possibly because unlike its predecessor it was brought about without any blood-letting) enabled the new Government in 1689 to pass the Toleration Act, whereby complete freedom of worship was granted to all Christians, who would subscribe to thirty six of the Thirty Nine articles, Roman Catholics and Unitarians alone of non-Anglican groups failing to benefit from the provisions of the Act. This Toleration Act, which attracted some criticism for not going far enough, at least assured the future spread of non-conformity in Wales, with the removal of all legal barriers to the establishment of denominational places of worship.

The Baptists were probably the first of the nonconformists sects to organise themselves in Wales; they, along with the Quakers and the Independents (Congregationalists) took advantage of the opportunities provided by the freer conditions of the early years of the Commonwealth. Readers will remember how, following the act of Parliament in 1650, which concerned itself with the propagation of the Gospel in Wales, two of the energetic itinerant preachers, appointed to see that the act's provisions were properly carried out, were Baptists, Hugh Evans and Vavasor Powell. Later Baptists, like other dissident groups, suffered in the 1660s from the rigorous laws, applied by the Church of England through their Members of Parliament, but after the short-lived Declaration of Indulgence, made by Charles II in 1672, a number of Baptist houses were officially recognised, where services could legally be held. After the passage of the Toleration Act in 1689, ushering in a new and more enlightened attitude towards differing Christian sects, considerable Baptist expansion soon took place in Wales, more particularly in the south of the country, where the first Baptist chapel was consecrated in the early 1690s at Llanwenarth, near Abergavenny.

The Independents followed a similar, if rather slower pattern of development; in 1639, as has already been mentioned, the very first nonconformist community in Wales was established at Llanfaches, near Newport. This Independent chapel however seems to have been an isolated development, arising from the personality of the former Anglican vicar of Llanfaches, whose liberal views caused his parishoners to turn him out. There was certainly some Congregationalist advance in Wales during the Commonwealth, but Congregationalism in Wales only really began to prosper in the freer religious atmosphere that followed the Toleration Act of 1689. The first Congregational chapel was built in 1692 at Rhayader, in the remote northern part of Radnorshire, where Congregationalist worshippers had previously met in a registered private house a few miles to the east in Nantmel. Four years later another Independent chapel was consecrated near Glasbury in south Radnorshire, known as Maes-yr-onnen, while, between these two early places of worship, in the eastern outskirts of what today is Llandrindod a Congregational chapel was erected in 1715. Caebach still serves the community thereabouts.

The Quakers (originally their enemies' name for them, which in the course of time, such was their courage and integrity, became an acceptable and respected alternative for their official name of *The Friends*) were amongst the earliest nonconformist sects to establish themselves in Wales. In 1654, two Radnorshire Quakers wrote to

George Fox, the founder of the movement, to invite him to visit them in central Wales, where their movement was thriving. In 1657, Fox accepted the invitation and was met by a great throng of interested men and women, who, previously advised of his coming, had gathered on Pen-y-bont Common near Llandegley in Radnorshire, where some stood, while others stayed on horseback to listen to Fox, who spoke to them for three hours. He paid further visits to the district in 1663 and 1666, as the Quaker cause prospered, despite increasing persecution.

In 1673 a farmer died, who had been in the original outdoor congregation in 1657; in his will he left a piece of land nearby, which was to be consecrated as a Quaker burial ground (The Pales) at a time, of course, when nonconformists were denied burial in consecrated ground. Six years later a Quaker meeting, which was in progress, either in the burial ground or in a building nearby, was raided by the High Sheriff of the county, who arrested all twelve members of the congregation, who were thereafter abused, maltreated, fined and imprisoned. Meanwhile there were many further Quaker conversions in central Wales, the new Quakers meeting in widely-separated safe houses.

In 1681 something unexpected happened, when the wealthy young son of Admiral Penn, was expelled from Oxford for being a Quaker; William thereupon emigrated to America, where he bought a piece of land, which he named Pennsylvania in honour of his father and there established a Quaker connection, which soon became a focal point for many Quakers in England, who sought freedom to practise their own religion. Amongst these emigrants were many from Wales, especially from Radnorshire, whose meetings for a while in consequence were much diminished. Quite how serious was the persecution of Quakers in England and Wales at this time can be seen from these figures; between 1650 and 1688 fourteen thousand suffered imprisonment, of whom three hundred and sixty nine died in prison.

Back in Radnorshire in 1717 on a piece of land, which adjoined the Pales' burial ground, a Meeting House was built, which today still caters for the needs of Quakers; it is the oldest such meeting house in Wales, in uninterrupted use. The GR is 138641; it will be found, with the aid of an Ordnance Survey map, near Llandegley, which is on the A44, between Kington and Rhayader.

B
f. Notes and Illustrations
A Sturdy Welsh Puritan

Briton Ferry in south Glamorgan was the birthplace in 1590 of John ap Henry, who in early adulthood, finding little prospect of earning his living locally, did what many of his fellow Welshmen did and migrated to London to make his way in the world. It is known that early on he became a servant in a Welsh family in the capital, moving later to a domestic position in the household of Philip, the Earl of Pembroke, the Lord President of the Welsh Council. Later, in 1625, John Henry (the 'ap' seems to have been lost in London) moved into the King's employment at Whitehall, where he became Keeper of the Orchard; his house, which went with the job, was near the Garden Steps, where, in addition to his responsibilities as a gardener, he was also required to help all visitors, as they embarked or disembarked at the much-frequented Garden Steps.

In 1631 a son was born, who was named Philip, after his father's former employer, the Earl of Pembroke. King Charles I had two sons, the future Charles II, born the previous year in 1630, and James, the future James II, born in 1633, both of whom became the constant playmates of the young Philip Henry, who all his life was to treasure a book given to him in boyhood by the younger brother, the Duke of York.

In the seventeenth century, when the river Thames was the main highway of London, the landing places were of considerable importance, none more so than the Garden Steps at Whitehall, which were to loom large in the life of the young Philip. The gathering clouds of political discord between the King and his Parliament gave rise to civil war in 1642; the very next year Philip Henry, now twelve years old, was entered at Westminster School, where he was to remain for the next four years. School became for the youthful Philip a peaceful oasis in those troubled times; his Headmaster, the famous Dr Busby thought highly of his Welsh

CONWY CASTLE

After the Statute of Rhuddlan in 1284 Edward I set about fortifying the coast of north Wales in an attempt to hold down the local people. At Conwy one thousand five hundred craftsmen and their labourers constructed a truly magnificent castle, whose defences were to be well tested more than three hundred years later, when at the outbreak of the Civil War John Williams, who had been born in the town, fled from York, where he had been enthroned as Archbishop, and returned home to Conwy. The castle had a chequered career between 1642 and 1646, as John Williams was ousted by his rival John Owen, whom Prince Rupert favoured. In 1646 Williams switched his allegiance from the King to Parliament and helped Colonel Mytton, the Parliamentary leader, to capture the town and castle. Within twenty years, in the early days of the restoration of the monarchy, the castle, once again in royal hands, was officially stripped of its iron and lead and most of its timbers, thus rapidly becoming the ruin, which still stands above the estuary in all its magnificence.

pupil, coming to regard him as an outstandingly able scholar. Indeed in 1647 Philip won a scholarship to Christ Church, Oxford, receiving as a leaving present from his father's former employer, the Earl of Pembroke, a gift of £10, which in his diary he gratefully acknowledged to be "a seasonable mercy".

Going into residence at Christ Church in October 1647, Philip was at once confronted with the need to answer a difficult question, on the answer to which his future career at the university depended. This indeed was the moment of decision; Parliament had won the Civil War and had every intention of rooting out all supporters of the defeated Royalist cause. Hence at the beginning of term all members of the University were compelled to reply to the question: "Will you submit to Parliament in the present visitation?" Philip managed to placate his interviewer by making this tactful reply. "I submit" he said "as far as I may with a safe conscience and without perjury".

A year later, shortly before Christmas 1648, he qualified for a vacation in London, where he was able to stay for some weeks with his father, who still lived near the Garden Steps in Whitehall. At the end of January 1649, while Philip was still at home, his father's employer, Charles I was executed, Philip, a sad witness of the event, commenting thus to his diary:

> " . . . The blow I saw given and can truly say with a sad heart; at that instant whereof there was such a groan by the thousands there present as I never heard before and desire I may never hear again."

Back at Christ Church he resumed his studies, first taking his Master's degree before being ordained in the Church of England in 1651. The offer of employment Philip was eagerly waiting for came in September 1653, when he was invited to visit Emral Hall in Flintshire, where he would be interviewed by Judge Puleston, who had the gift of the living of Worthenbury. Philip's host, Judge Puleston had been a loyal supporter of the Parliamentary cause in the tumultuous times of the 1640s, and as reward for his services had been made a Judge after the death of the King in 1649.

Philip for his part was most certainly a Royalist up to the time that he went up to Oxford; in the difficult early days of the Commonwealth he seems to have kept to himself any doubts he may have felt about politics and religion. At Emral Hall on the occasion of this all-important interview he met the Judge, whose loyalty to Parliament had never been in doubt and his wife, who not only shared her husband's views but was also a tireless and persuasive advocate of the Parliamentary cause.

The young Philip having enjoyed the hospitality of the Pulestons and been introduced to their five sons, eagerly accepted the Judge's offer to preach in Worthenbury church and to act as tutor to his five sons, for which he was to get an annual stipend of £60 and receive free board and lodging in Emral Hall, where he would be treated as one of the family.

While Philip Henry was serving his professional apprenticeship as a preacher, great changes were taking place in church and state. The monarchy had been abolished and the republican commonwealth had taken its place, with Oliver Cromwell leading the nation. Parliament ruled supreme. In matters of religion local committees had been set up, which were authorised to appoint parish priests, who in the next few years came to represent just about every possible shade of Protestant opinion.

In Worthenbury, Judge Puleston was very tolerant towards dissent, while Lady Puleston was positively enthusiastic about it. Against this contemporary background of religious experimentation, Philip Henry settled down to fulfil his dual role of parish priest and tutor to the Judge's sons. In 1655, the Judge showed his approval of his protégé by increasing his stipend to £100 per annum; in 1656 the eldest boy, Roger was enrolled in his tutor's old college, Christ Church. From that time there was growing evidence of a widening rift between Philip and Roger, who also fell out with his mother (probably for doctrinal reasons, as Lady Puleston's Puritan tendencies found less and less favour with her eldest son, who was deeply attached to the traditional beliefs of the Church of England). In that same year Philip confided to his diary a deep sense of shame; apparently, in the course of a difference of opinion with Roger, the latter lost his temper and struck his tutor, who retaliated by slapping the young man's face. Later, in 1657 a seemingly anomalous situation arose when Philip, the Rector of Worthenbury, was also ordained as Presbyterian Minister of Prees.

1658 and 1659 were years of doubt and misfortune for Philip Henry. The first blow fell in September when his champion, Lady Puleston died; Philip took the funeral service and preached the sermon, later that day lamenting in his diary that "she was the best friend I had on earth". The following February Philip moved out from Emral Hall into the Rectory at Worthenbury, which the Judge had had specially built for him. Later that same year the second blow fell, when the Judge himself died; thus the new baronet was Roger, who was a staunch upholder of the Church of England and an implacable enemy of the Rector. The restoration of the monarchy in 1660 brought everything to a head locally in Worthenbury, leading to open hostility between patron and priest, between Sir Roger Puleston and his old tutor, whose nonconformist attitude seemed to increase as his patron's heart hardened against him.

The difficult situation was inflamed by Philip's refusal to read in church from the Book of Common Prayer, to which Sir Roger reacted by refusing to pay Philip's stipend. Philip, after repeating his offence of not reading from the Prayer Book, twice found himself brought up at the Flintshire Assizes, the consequences of which were that he agreed to take an oath of allegiance to King Charles II but refused to submit himself, as required, for reordination. Hence on October 26th 1661 Sir Roger Puleston, acting on instructions from his Bishop, had Philip Henry ejected from Worthenbury. In 1662, Parliament legalised this and other similar actions elsewhere by passing the Act of Uniformity. Thus cast out, Philip Henry passed the remaining thirty-five years of his life, ploughing a very lonely furrow as a staunch and very determined Puritan. Some readers may care to know that 2 months after this ejection his first son, Matthew was born, who twenty five years later became a Presbyterian minister in Chester. This

THE SHIRE HALL, PRESTEIGNE

In this view of Presteigne today the Shire Hall can be seen on the left-hand side; here in the 1640s (Presteigne at that time being the county town) the leading Radnorshire Baptist, Vavasor Powell appeared to answer a charge; the building, seen in the photograph, was erected in 1829.

QUAKER MEETING-HOUSE, THE PALES, LLANDEGLEY

This remote place of worship, still in regular use, was built in 1717 and remains much as it was a hundred and fifty and more years ago. Under the thatched roof will be found two rooms, one for Quaker worship, the other used for a display of Quaker literature, all set out on a hand-bier.

Matthew Henry was to achieve great fame as a leader of nonconformist thought.

Lhuyd of the Ashmolean (1660-1709)

Most of the seventeenth century, it has already been seen, was devoted to constitutional issues, which led to serious internal dissension and civil war, culminating in the temporary abolition of monarchy; the disastrous quarrel broke out again in the second half of the century and only found its solution in the last decade of the century. After the 1688 settlement, however, with its insistence on the future supremacy of Parliament, and the prospect of better times ahead, signs appeared which suggested the possible dawn of a new age, signs which had previously been stunted and delayed by the social and political upheavals earlier in the century. Changes, when they come, do not of course happen suddenly; it is one of the advantages that accrue from studying the past that new developments, new ways of thinking can be seen in their historical context. The future never lies ahead of us, said Confucius, but always comes flying over our heads from behind.

Soon after the restoration of the monarchy in Charles II's reign, at a time when religious bigotry was once again rearing its ugly head, scholars in universities were beginning to realise the virtue of working together in the common interest of acquiring new knowledge, more particularly in connection with scientific ideas. Indeed the growth of modern organised scientific research can be traced back to the early years of Charles II's reign, when the King himself gave his approval and his patronage to the Royal Society, which was founded in 1663; it was the first scientific society in this country and one of the first in Europe.

In a wider sense, however, this Royal Society can be seen to have had its roots in the Renaissance, which had given rise to a new and welcome spirit of enquiry in Western Europe. If in London this spirit of enquiry had found belated expression in the Royal Society, in Wales it had already inspired the antiquarian movement, whose foremost and most distinguished contributor, Robert Vaughan of

Hengwrt in Merionethshire, caused it to flourish in the seventeenth century. When he died in 1667, there were on hand other Welshmen ready and able to take on where Vaughan had left off. Such a man was Edward Lhuyd.

Lhuyd was born to Welsh parents near Oswestry in 1660; he was educated at Oswestry Grammar School before going up to Jesus College, Oxford the alma mater for generations of Welshmen past and present. He had already developed a lively interest in heraldry and genealogy, and on arrival at Oxford opted to study geology and botany, with what success is not known because he left the university without taking a degree. In 1684, however, his path crossed that of Elias Ashmole, an antiquary who had spent many years collecting curios; in old age he presented his collection to Oxford University on condition that a suitable museum was built to house his exhibits. The outcome was the Ashmolean Museum, which in fact was the first such public museum in this country; in 1684 Lhuyd was appointed its Assistant Keeper.

Before long the Assistant Keeper was back in Wales, exhaustively collecting on behalf of the museum fossils and plants; something of his enthusiasm and thoroughness can be gauged from the fact that on Snowdon alone he managed to identify thirty-seven plants, which were not native to these islands, among them the exceedingly rare Mountain Spiderwort, a white flower with purple-red veins, which thereafter bore his name, *Lloydia Serotina*. In 1686, he was back at the Ashmolean in Oxford, busily sorting, collating and preparing his material for his first book, which was published in 1699; this book dealt mainly with fossils, though his remarkable plant findings were listed earlier in the works of others. Edward Lhuyd was already an acknowledged naturalist.

Having, as it were, served his apprenticeship at the Ashmolean as an Assistant, Lhuyd set out upon his life's main work, fortified by his appointment as the Keeper of the Museum. From 1697 to 1701 he was to travel continually on behalf of the museum, his ambitions, archaeological and linguistic. His ultimate goal was to compile an *Archaeologia Britannica* but, as he became more and more immersed in his enthusiastic work in the field, his interest in fossils and bones, in plants and in sites of archaeological importance gradually became subordinated to a greater awareness of the over-riding need to make a full study of all the Celtic languages, their grammar, their vocabularies and their cultures. This all-consuming interest was to involve him in journeys to Ireland and Scotland, to Cornwall and Brittany, as well, of course as innumerable visits to Wales. Over the years vast quantities of future museum exhibits were packed up and sent back to Oxford, rocks and fossils, plants and detailed plans and drawings of archaeological sites, while all the time he continued to soak himself in Celtic languages.

Travel in these largely unvisited places was at this time uncomfortable, difficult and sometimes dangerous, as when Lhuyd saw the inside of a Breton prison, as a suspected spy! Wherever he went, he asked questions and took copious notes, which happily survive and are still of real value. Two examples must suffice to show just how great a debt modern students owe to him for his thoroughness and his insistence on writing down everything of interest which came his way.

Readers in the Llangollen area of north Wales will be familiar with Eliseg's Pillar, which stands in a field, some two miles north of the town, near the ruins of the Vallé Crucis monastery; it is the oldest (ninth century) and most important field monument of its kind in the whole of Wales. Originally it was a cross, which so impressed the Cistercians when they came to the district to build their monastery that they remembered it in giving it a name. Unfortunately posterity and the elements have together dealt harshly with the monument but on the credit side, when Edward Lhuyd visited it, the inscription, incised on the shaft, was still mostly visible. Hence, with Lhuyd's help, we may still learn something of the history of the early rulers of Powys.

Further south, in Llanddewi Brefi, four miles south of Tregaron, is one of the most historically interesting churches in Wales, with its association with St David himself, to whom it is dedicated. Today high up on the outside north-west wall of the nave can just be detected an early Christian memorial stone. Less

QUAKER BURIAL GROUND, THE PALES, LLANDEGLEY
In the last quarter of the 17th century this burial ground was consecrated; the earliest surviving gravestones date from 1838 (Quaker graves remained unmarked until 1830). Today there are just over 70 stones in this welltended burial ground, which is hewn out of the side of the Radnor Forest. It is joined through a little gate to the rest of the Quaker settlement.

MAES-YR-ONNEN CHAPEL
In 1696, seven years after the Toleration Act allowed nonconformists to have their own places of worship, this Independent chapel was consecrated. Though remotely situated, it can be easily approached from the A438 road from Brecon to Hereford, near Glasbury in south Radnorshire. (G.R. 177411). The chapel happily is still in use.

than half of the original Idnert Stone survives, but, when Lhuyd passed that way in the 1690s, it was intact and, of course, he made a copy of the Latin inscription, which had originally marked the churchyard grave of the murdered Idnert, the Abbot of the monastery of Llanbadarn Fawr (near Aberystwyth); this inscription, which dates from the seventh century, has the added interest of containing the earliest known reference to St David.

Sometime in 1701 Lhuyd returned to the Ashmolean Museum, where he started the long and arduous task of organising and collating his material, preparatory to setting about the massive task which he had set himself. The first volume of this *Archaeologia Britannica* was eventually published in 1707; it marked the beginning of a new academic approach, that of comparative philology, whereby the grammars, the vocabularies, the syntaxes of the various Celtic languages studied were described, analysed and compared. This book was the first scientific enquiry into the Celtic languages, and its publication assured its author of the status of an outstanding Celtic scholar. His old university rewarded him with an honorary Master of Arts degree, but in 1708 he received the supreme accolade of scholarship, when he was made a Fellow of the Royal Society.

Anticlimax tragically was to follow because his health broke down; the many hardships which he had had to endure on the many strenuous journeys he had undertaken in distant places and always regardless of the weather, had undermined his ability to resist disease. Asthma, followed by pleurisy, sapped his vitality; furthermore, though he received the highest academic recognition, he continued to exist on a meagre stipend. The resultant poverty, allied with chronic pleurisy, brought about his premature death, in 1709, before his fiftieth birthday and before any more of the other projected volumes could be written.

To summarise, Edward Lhuyd was a very great Celtic scholar, a pioneer in Celtic philological studies, and a pathfinder to those as yet unborn to whom his studies would point the way to future scientific enquiries into Celtic culture.

ELISEG'S PILLAR

Originally sixteen feet high, it was put up in the first half of the 9th century by Cyngen to honour the memory of his great grandfather, Eliseg, who had ruled Powys in the early years of the eighth century. In the seventeenth century it was cruelly buffeted in the Civil War and by subsequent Puritan prejudice, although enough of it survived for Edward Lhuyd in 1696 to be able to make a note of the original inscription. It was re-erected in its present form in 1779.

A Seventeenth Century Church

For those who like to envisage past events happening against an actual historical background, like watching a play unfold in front of well-designed scenery on the stage, a visit to a seventeenth century church is not only a useful visual aid to the understanding of past events, but also a spur to the imagination, without which some studies of the past tend to become too arid and too academic for many readers. In this connection it is as well to remember that there were notable churchmen in Wales at this time as well as dissidents, though the latter seem in after years to have attracted most attention. When therefore, seeing in the mind's eye religious observances in a seventeenth century church, think, if you will, of a man like Huw Morus; he hailed from the Ceiriog Valley, where an obelisk marks his birthplace at Pont-y-meibion and he worshipped at Llansilin church, in southern Denbighshire, in whose churchyard he was buried. Readers of George Borrow may recall that the English traveller in 1854 persuaded the local inn-keeper in Llansilin to show him the grave, whereupon the Englishman proceeded to kneel down and kiss the cold stone. Morus, an outstanding poet of his times, was always a devout Anglican, who supported the King's side in the Civil War, but later quarrelled with James II because he the King no longer upheld the Church of England!

A seventeenth century church happily survives in Radnorshire, at Disserth, which lies about two miles south-west of Llandrindod (GR 034583). There is no village, the church and a farm comprising Disserth, which, deriving its name from the Latin desertum, indicated a suitable place for a hermitage, which is where St Cewydd, a sixth century Christian missionary, first established himself. Today's church, dedicated to the same early Christian missionary, stands near the river Ithon; it was built in the Middle Ages on the original site and largely restored in the seventeenth century, but had the great good fortune to escape further restoration in Victorian times, with the happy result that the interior today is very much as it was three hundred and more

LLANDDEWI BREFI CHURCH

St David's church stands on a mound, which may suggest to archaeologists a Bronze Age settlement many centuries before the dawn of Christianity; to others however, more romantically inclined, the mound brings back memories of the legend, given prominence by Rhigfarch, the eleventh century biographer of St David, who reported that David as a young man had been present at an outdoor synod there, where he had spoken with such eloquence and authority that the very ground had risen up! Certain it is that a few centuries earlier still the Romans had settled in the neighbourhood, on the other side of the river, Teifi, at Pontllanio.

years ago; the box pews are still in place, many of them still bearing the names of their seventeenth century occupants, their arrangement a vivid illustration of the social structure of the time. In addition the triple-decker pulpit also belonged to the seventeenth century, while on the wall can still be faintly seen the royal arms of Charles II.

Bearing in mind the Stuart insistence on the divinity of kings, it is hardly surprising that the ancient royal belief in the King's ability to cure diseased subjects, if they were only allowed to touch the royal person, was popular with the Stuarts. This quaint custom, which seems to have been begun in the twelfth century in the reign of Henry II, was at its most popular in the reign of Charles II, who is reputed to have allowed more than ninety thousand sick subjects to touch him in order to be cured of scrofula (an earlier name for tuberculosis). Here in Disserth there survived on a wall of the church, well into the nineteenth century, a proclamation, dated 1683, which informed sick parishoners where they had to go and when, if they wanted to be cured of what was then called "the King's evil".

Readers will know how important a part wells have played in the customs and folk-lore of rural Wales; Disserth was no exception and, when Edward Lhuyd visited the district in 1698, he talked with a local woman, who informed him that women still decorated the local well on New Year's Eve with mistletoe, in the sure hope that the New Year might look with favour upon them. This local custom apparently still survived at the beginning of the twentieth century.

DISSERTH CHURCH

On the north side of the churchyard, which was unconsecrated, parishoners, even up to the beginning of the twentieth century, frequently made merry, as they were quite entitled to do, as this part of the churchyard was regarded as the village playground. Here at Disserth, as at many another place in Wales, the annual patronal feast was celebrated with such secular activities as eating, drinking, playing games and dancing, activities which, when the weather turned wet, were generally transferred to the nave of the church.

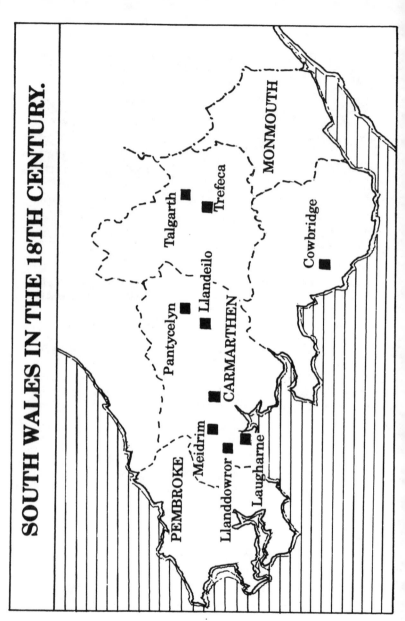

SOUTH WALES IN THE 18TH CENTURY.

MONMOUTH

Cowbridge

Trefeca

Talgarth

Llandeilo

CARMARTHEN

Pantycelyn

Meidrim

Laugharne

Llanddowror

PEMBROKE

Part III
Developments in the Eighteenth Century

At the end of the seventeenth century, a century of religious, social and economic turmoil, there was a need above all for a period of consolidation, especially as England was about to be ruled by a new dynasty from abroad whose members could make no pretence of believing in the divine right of kings, when they had been invited to London by mere human beings! The century that followed in England was politically dull and unexciting; in London Parliament, to whom power had passed in the revolutionary settlement of 1688, needed time to feel its feet. Wales, for its part, may still have lain, largely undigested in the belly of England, yet, for the time being, seemed unwilling or unable to kick against its masters. In fact, at this time many leading Welshmen, having allowed themselves to become thoroughly anglicised, probably thought the outlook in the new century very promising in terms of career prospects. Nevertheless, though politically little was stirring in eighteenth-century Wales, in other and equally important spheres of life things were beginning to move. In the course of the century significant educational reforms and even more significant religious changes took place; however, something has first to be said about one very important aspect of Welsh economic life and at the end of the chapter, when the educational and religious developments have been described, it will be necessary to introduce the reader to some new ideological thinking that spread in Wales towards the end of the century, as revolutionary ideas began to inspire men of action in France.

a. Economic
Of all the branches of government into which academics tend to divide up our lives, none is so calculated to raise a yawn as economic; lest readers of this book should agree, let me hasten to reassure them because this economic section is one of the most interesting as well as being one of the most important parts of this

chapter, simply and solely because enthusiasts, Ordnance maps in hand, can spend many happy holidays tracing the drovers' roads, for which a great deal of visual evidence survives. Actual stretches of roads, inns, cider houses and groups of Scots pine trees, may all be seen in true historical context.

Where there are mountains there are valleys; on mountain slopes sheep graze, while cattle graze down below. From the early years of the Middle Ages sheep and cattle provided Welsh farmers with a livelihood, whenever they were able to get their beasts to market — preferably in the more populous areas of England. The strong black cattle that flourished in Wales were probably the first to plod their long, hard way eastwards, later to be joined by sheep, later still by geese and pigs, and in the eighteenth century by turkeys.

For a long time this passage of cattle eastwards through Wales was probably quite haphazard, but gradually, as the trade grew and prospered, the values of co-operation became obvious. Thereafter, from Anglesey in the north to Pembrokeshire in the south, herds of cattle congregated at pre-arranged places, before starting the long trek together. Resting places were agreed upon, where the drove masters could find suitable and comfortable places to stay, and their assistants adequate if less expensive, bivouacs, where the herds could be fed and watered and when necessary, reshod in conveniently located smithies. Today many a former drovers' inn will be found to have as neighbour a one-time forge.

After the Act of Union this increasingly important drovers' trade became properly organised; as a general rule herds were divided into sections of about four hundred cattle, for whose welfare twelve men were responsible. These assistants accompanied their charges on foot, but the drove masters usually rode ponies, and at their side scampered the quite invaluable corgi dogs. It was at this juncture, in the middle of the sixteenth century, that Parliament began to legislate in this matter; laws passed in the reigns of Edward VI and Elizabeth required a drove master, who had to be relicensed every year, to be a married man and a house-owner, as well as being at least thirty years of age. A century later, civil war in the 1640s presented a serious threat to the drovers, but towards the end of the century the trade expanded very rapidly, as the gentlemen of England in their country houses discovered that their guests greatly appreciated the 'roast beef of old England' — imported from Wales!

The drove masters, the bosses on horseback, had much to arrange before setting out on their long journey to the east; they had to budget for the expenses that would accrue, the payment for accommodation for themselves in inns, for their assistants in farm-houses or in barns, for fodder and pasture for the herds, and, by no means least, for the re-shoeing of their cattle, which was usually necessary several times in the course of their long trek. These drove masters were often men of substance, and were certainly held in high esteem. Their acquaintance was thought worth cultivating by inn-keepers, farmers and blacksmiths. Farmers, anxious to attract attention, often indicated their willingness to provide pasture and accommodation by planting clusters of Scots pine trees at the approach to the farm. The public generally in Wales also came to regard the drove masters as something of an institution, which could be trusted. People with relatives living in England trusted the drovers to deliver letters to them; many went much further and gave them sums of money to be handed over, maybe, to a son in an English university or in an inn of court in London. Often too drovers were given money for the repayment of a debt in England. So frequent were these calls made on the drovers that they gradually arranged with safe houses back in Wales to look after the money for them; this happened especially in the eighteenth century when it was more dangerous to travel with money, as highway robbery became a much greater problem. In such cases the drovers would then, once they had sold their cattle in England (and sometimes their ponies too, causing them to have to walk home!) hand over equivalent sums of money to creditors or waiting sons out of the proceeds of their financial transactions. On their return to Wales the drovers would reimburse themselves from their 'safe houses', which in the course of time became private banks, one of the best known of which was the Black Ox at Llandovery.

By the eighteenth century, which was the heyday of the drovers' activities, about nine thousand cattle a year headed east from Anglesey, while as many as twenty thousand were thought to leave Pembrokeshire every year for the English market, some thirteen thousand of which passed through Herefordshire. In the course of this century the routine of the drovers was considerably affected by the great increase in the number of non-conformists in Wales, who threatened eternal damnation to those who worked on Sunday. In consequence Sunday became a compulsory day of rest for all drovers and their cattle, necessitating drastic changes in their arrangements. Great apparently was the activity to be observed in many country places on Sunday nights as midnight approached! Penalties exacted against those who failed to heed the Sabbath were very heavy indeed. Also in this second half of this eighteenth century there came into existence the first turnpike roads along which at intervals tollgates were set up, where money had to be paid by those who used the roads. Drovers — and there were many of them — who wanted to escape this extra expense, tended to leave the roads and take their herds over hill and dale. By the end of the century, despite these unexpected changes, the drovers' activities had been accepted as economically very necessary; successful drovers became prosperous and important members of society. It was ironical therefore that this widespread acknowledgement of success should have been so suddenly followed by their rapid decline, because in the early years of the nineteenth century the coming of the railways provided a very different and a very much speedier solution to the problem of getting cattle to market. Over the centuries so many cattle were driven from Wales into England on so many different routes that a selection has to be made if the text is to be kept within reasonable limits. Hence it is proposed to deal with five much-used drovers' routes, covering the whole of Wales, in the hope that these outlines and their maps may give a fair general picture of this very important social and economic activity.

Route I: From North-west Wales to Wrexham

The herds from Anglesey and the Llŷn Peninsula, having joined up near Pren-teg, (not far from where Porthmadog is today), and been marshalled, used to take off for Maentwrog en route for Ffestiniog; next they crossed the moors to Ysbyty Ifan before they reached Pentrefoelas, where they would be joined by more cattle, coming there from further north. At Cerrigydrudion about six miles east of Pentrefoelas, there was usually a very necessary stop for re-shoeing. From there a popular route again lay across moorland, this time to Ruthin, where several drovers' routes met. In fact Ruthin was a drovers' town, where much accommodation was available. There was a popular Drovers' Arms to the north of the town, while four miles to the south on the road to Llanfair Dyffryn Clwyd, there was a hostelry, well-known to drovers, known as the Three Pigeons. Thereafter the final stage to Wrexham generally passed through Llanarmon-yn-Iâl.

Route 2: From Dolgellau to Llangollen

The coastal districts to the north-west of Dolgellau were a very important catchment area for cattle; from Dolgellau many cattle were driven inland up the hilly road which led to Bala, roughly corresponding to the modern A494 via Rhyd-y-main. After Bala a much-traversed route lay via Llandderfel, Llandrillo and Cynwyd to Corwen, where a number of drovers' routes met; from Corwen the most straightforward way to Llangollen was similar to the one the A5 takes today.

Route 3: From Machynlleth to Shrewsbury

From medieval times Machynlleth has been a cattle-grazing centre; even before Owain Glyndŵr in the opening decade of the fifteenth century brought fame to the town (he made it the capital of Wales) Machynlleth held important cattle markets in the spring and autumn. From the town the drovers' route climbed south-east up the Dulas valley to Staylittle, where more cattle joined the drove from Llanbryn-mair, further north. Thus augmented, the herd

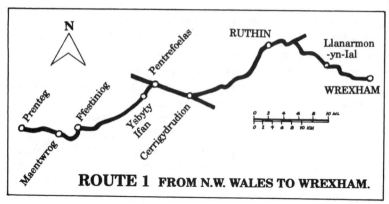

ROUTE 1 FROM N.W. WALES TO WREXHAM.

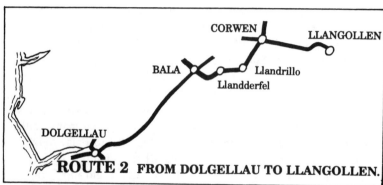

ROUTE 2 FROM DOLGELLAU TO LLANGOLLEN.

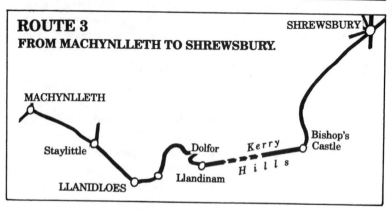

ROUTE 3
FROM MACHYNLLETH TO SHREWSBURY.

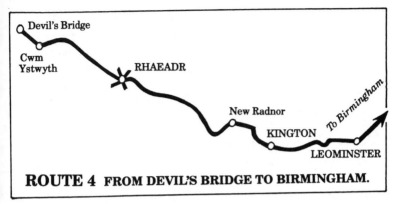

ROUTE 4 FROM DEVIL'S BRIDGE TO BIRMINGHAM.

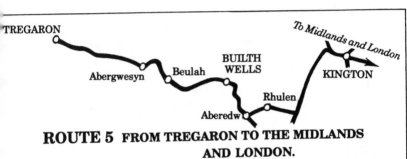

ROUTE 5 FROM TREGARON TO THE MIDLANDS
AND LONDON.

trudged its way to Llanidloes, which, then as now, was a farming area of some consequence. There was a choice of routes for drovers moving east of Llanidloes, one of which went north-east to Llandinam before turning in an easterly direction, keeping to the south of Newtown and crossing over the Kerry Hills into Shropshire, where a choice of markets from Shrewsbury southwards beckoned to them.

Route 4: From Devil's Bridge to Birmingham

The area around Devil's Bridge has long been a cattle centre, which necessitated the establishment there of an essential local industry, devoted to providing suitable footwear for the cattle, who migrated from there to the east in great numbers. Many drovers chose to drive their herds eastwards to Cwmyswyth, from where they set out over the hills, thus approaching Rhayader from the north-west. Rhayader, which has been a thriving market town ever since the Middle Ages, was conveniently situated for the drovers, many of whom, after leaving the town in a south-easterly direction more or less anticipated the line of the future A44, through Crossgates and Kington to Leominster, and on to Birmingham.

Route 5: From Tregaron to the Midlands and London

Further to the south is Tregaron, today, as for centuries, a busy market town, giving access to the most picturesque of all drovers' routes over the Cambrian Mountains to the east of the town. Modern visitors to Tregaron, who want to absorb something of the historical atmosphere of the place, would do well to have a leisurely meal in the Talbot Arms, in the main square. In this former favourite calling place for drove masters George Borrow stayed in the 1850s, and it was here that he was assured that "Tregaron is not quite so big as London but is a very good place". Sheep and cattle from south and south-east of the town for centuries assembled near the Talbot Arms, there to be shod before setting out on the daunting climb up into the mountains to the east.

The road today from Tregaron to Abergwesyn is quite feasible for cars, if care is taken, especially when negotiating the tight bends on the Devil's Staircase; the hills here are remote and beautiful and silent. True lovers of the wild should make the journey at least once, preferably travelling from west to east, as the drovers had to do. After Abergwesyn, the route lay through Beulah and then down to the Wye at Builth, turning east up the Edw Valley a few miles south of Builth. Between Aberedw and Kington, if readers want to keep strictly to the way the drovers' went, consult an ordnance maps and make sure to include a stop at the little white-washed church at Rhulen, before making use of more modern roads to Kington, Leominster and places further east and south. Readers who want to find out more about the drovers and their times are strongly recommended to read *The Drovers' Roads of Wales* by Fay Godwin and Shirley Toulson.

b. Educational

General illiteracy had become apparent in Wales towards the end of the sixteenth century, when it became clear that many could not read Bishop Morgan's Welsh Bible. A few years earlier the lone voice of John Penry had been raised in protest against the ignorance and poverty of so many of his fellow countrymen. Nothing much however seems to have been done to improve matters until the early years of the Commonwealth, when in 1650 Parliament passed the Act for the Better Propagation of the Gospel, one result of which was the establishment in Wales of a number of schools for the children of parishes, attached to churches, which helped to maintain them in part from their tithes. The curriculum was mostly devoted to reading, writing and arithmetic and, believe it or believe it not, some Latin, but no Welsh. This absence of Welsh helps to explain the lack of success, which attended this otherwise useful experiment, which was to come to a full-stop, when the status quo was restored by the restoration of the monarchy in 1660.

Twelve years later, in 1672, would-be reformers were given another chance when Charles II unexpectedly proclaimed (for political reasons) a Declaration of Indulgence, which marked the beginning of a short-lived period of toleration, of which a certain ejected London Puritan took full advantage. Thomas Gouge, who had been ejected from St Sepulchre's church in Southwark, had paid his first visit to Wales in 1671, when, in the course of an illegal preaching tour he had been struck by the large number of destitute and quite illiterate Welsh people. He thereupon took the decision to set up schools in Wales and returned hotfoot to London to appeal for the necessary financial help, which he seems to have done so successfully that in 1674 he established the Welsh Trust. He was to have an important ally in this work, a Welshman, Stephen Hughes, who too had been ejected — from Meidrim in Carmarthenshire. This Stephen Hughes had independently of Gouge for some time been thinking and working along similar lines. He had already translated into Welsh the Catechism, the Book of Psalms and the Book of Common Prayer; indeed it was on a visit to London to get his translations published that Hughes met Gouge and the fortunate and fruitful partnership was formed.

In the Trust, along with ejected Puritans like Gouge and Hughes were orthodox Anglican priests like Tillotson and Stillingfleet, (both destined later to become bishops), as well as Nonconformists like Richard Baxter. Of the outstanding contribution made by Gouge to this movement pride of place must go to his success in building a bridge, at least during the early years, between those who had been thrown out of the Church of England and those who had chosen to stay inside. This Welsh Trust, which enjoyed the financial patronage of the Lord Mayor of London and his Aldermen, seems to have had two main objects, to pay for the publication and the distribution of Welsh Christian literature to the Welsh, and to establish free schools for Welsh children, the so-called charity schools. Stephen Hughes above all showed the way in translating suitable books into Welsh and in supervising their printing and their subsequent distribution, the climax of his achievement coming in 1678, when a thousand copies of a newly-published edition of Morgan's Bible were given to those in Wales who needed them most. The considerable expense involved in this and other religious publications during these years was jointly borne by Anglicans and Nonconformists.

That this Welsh Trust, with its wholly admirable aims and intentions, lasted for so short a time, (it virtually came to an end when Thomas Gouge died in 1681) must above all be attributed to the seemingly illogical obstinacy of most members of the Trust's Board, who, while encouraging Stephen Hughes to feed Welsh minds with books in Welsh, yet steadfastly demanded that all education in their charity schools should be conducted solely in the English language. Reliable facts and figures are not easy to come by, but it seems that at its peak the Trust had eighty seven schools open in Wales. Gouge's death in 1681 coincided with the abandonment by Charles II of any tolerance towards Nonconformists; sterner times for minorities lay ahead in the immediate future. All the same, this Welsh Trust did provide a link in an educational chain, which had been forged in the years of the Commonwealth. When at the end of the seventeenth century, a new voluntary educational development took shape, the new men, as will be seen, were able to build upon some of the foundations laid by Thomas Gouge and Stephen Hughes.

When the Society for the Promotion of Christian Knowledge came into being in 1699, it owed a very great deal to the pioneering work of the Welsh Trust, most of whose leaders had vanished from the scene, many of them dying with a quite unmerited sense of failure. Men like Gouge and Hughes laboured long and hard in their cause, their posthumous contribution being of considerable value to the founders of the new movement. The S.P.C.K., however, limited its membership to those who subscribed to the tenets of the Church of England, as there was no place for nonconformists in their ranks. There were a number of early members with strong Welsh associations, none more outstanding than Sir John Philipps, a Pembrokeshire landowner, who devoted all his energies and most of his fortune to the cause of the S.P.C.K.

Its aims were implicit in its title, its method to spread Christianity through publishing and distributing suitable religious tracts and books, and to set up, where the need was greatest, basic schools, where a knowledge of Christianity and the ability to read the Bible might be obtained. Its activities were organised on a territorial basis with each district having its own correspondent, who provided a link with headquarters in London. The early work of the S.P.C.K. was seriously hampered by a woeful shortage of clergy in Wales, a situation which encouraged pluralism. In these circumstances many a Welsh clergyman, not unreasonably, preferred a living with an adequate stipend east of Offa's Dyke to one, which barely guaranteed survival for his family in Wales. In addition, it has to be remembered that a very large number of Anglican livings in Wales were in the hands of secular landlords, some of whom often accepted no obligation to take into account either the spiritual needs of the parishoners or the physical well-being of the priest. To take an extreme example one lay patron, an English duke, obtained £900 per annum from rents in certain parishes in Carmarthenshire, out of which he contributed a mere £70 towards the annual stipends of the six curates, whom he appointed to do what little they could. Thus widespread and growing poverty in many parts of Wales meant that fewer and fewer parishes could be adequately served. In Anne's reign (1702-14) the good Queen did something through what became known as Queen Anne's Bounty, to ameliorate conditions for those Welsh priests, whose stipends amounted to less than £50 a year.

The S.P.C.K. like its predecessors in educational pioneering in Wales, had to face the language problem; their agreed general principle was to insist on English being the language of instruction, except where common sense suggested otherwise, — as in Welsh-speaking areas! The outcome was the widespread use of Welsh in the north of the country, and indeed in other parts where Welsh was in general use, while elsewhere, and particularly in the south-west, English prevailed. In these S.P.C.K. schools, ninety-six of which were set up between 1699 and 1740, all children had to learn to read and to write and to recite the catechism; the boys were also taught arithmetic, while the girls' curriculum concentrated on the imparting of knowledge of such domestic skills as needlework, knitting, spinning and weaving.

The most serious handicap faced by the schools was a shortage of teachers, for whom the basic qualifications were membership of the Church of England and a reasonable familiarity with the three Rs. The S.P.C.K. correspondent in Pembrokeshire, the admirable Sir John Philipps, sensing the problem, suggested the setting-up of a training college for teachers, but his appeal fell on deaf ears. At the heart of the problem was lack of money. Indeed the only funds accruing to the schools for their maintenance came from voluntary subscriptions, a few endowments and church collections. The S.P.C.K. itself could not afford to contribute money, though it did much to supply books, free of charge, where the need was greatest.

Of the ninety-six schools, sixty-eight were established by 1715; after 1727 a serious decline set in, which by 1740 had become terminal. While it is difficult to attempt to make an appraisal of these schools, they did at least maintain a certain continuity of educational effort, which was to have beneficial consequences in the long run. Of more long-lasting significance was the S.P.C.K.'s achievement in continuing to publish books in Welsh for adults. They also founded eight libraries (the first at Carmarthen) where Church of England priests were able to continue their education and widen their knowledge. Above all, it has to be remembered that it was one of the Society's teachers, who in later years mounted a most successful campaign against illiteracy in Wales, Gruffydd Jones.

Of the many outstanding Welshmen of the eighteenth century none sensed and supplied the needs of his fellow countrymen more accurately than did this Gruffydd Jones; from small beginnings as a parish priest who also taught in S.P.C.K. schools, he set in motion the most important educational movement of the eighteenth century, the circulating schools. The barebones of his career are these; born in 1683 in Carmarthen, where he went to school, he was ordained, without going to university, in 1708, became a curate at Laugharne, where he also taught in a S.P.C.K. school, later moving to Llandeilo, before being presented in 1716 by Sir John Philipps with the living at Llanddowror, where four years later he married his patron's sister. Gruffydd Jones was to spend the rest of his life as Vicar of Llanddowror, dying in 1761.

In his early days he had concentrated on being an evangelical preacher, frequently preaching out of his own parish, though always with the permission of the local vicar. By 1730, however, he felt the need for a change of direction and spent more time teaching people to read the Bible. Hence he rented a cottage in Llanddowror, where he organised short courses for would-be teachers; here he enrolled keen young men, who were allowed to join his classes provided that they were members of the Church of England and loyal supporters of George II. To these enthusiasts Jones imparted sufficient basic knowledge of rudimentary methods of teaching to enable his young men to go out into the schools which Gruffydd Jones was setting up and there teach the children their catechism. These missionary teachers, for such in fact they were, held their classes, wherever a suitable place was available, in church or barn, and in three months equipped the children as best they could. Gruffydd Jones was ever a realist; he knew that children would not be available in the summer months, when their labour would be required in the fields. Hence these three-monthly courses were organised between September and May, for the children in the daytime and their parents in the evenings, thereby laying the foundations of adult education.

In this, the first home-produced educational programme for Wales, Gruffydd Jones placed great emphasis on the use of the Welsh language; for the first time Welsh was insisted upon in all schools, even in the south, where it was certainly a new idea. That these circulating schools succeeded in their limited purpose cannot be denied, the most important single factor in their success being the personality of Gruffydd Jones himself. He was however exceptionally fortunate to enjoy the support of two extremely wealthy people, his patron and brother-in-law, Sir John Philipps and Bridget Beavan, the heiress wife of the Member of Parliament for Carmarthen. Bridget Beavan's generosity relieved Gruffydd Jones of any financial worry, enabling him to use all his own money, which mostly came from subscriptions in England, to provide salaries for his teachers. In addition, the S.P.C.K. continued to give the movement invaluable assistance by equipping all the circulating schools with books. When Gruffydd Jones died in 1761, Bridget took over full responsibility for maintaining all the schools; this she continued to do until she died eighteen years later, in which year there were two hundred and forty-three schools. These circulating schools indeed managed to survive well into the nineteenth century.

It is sad to have to report that throughout his long and honourable career, Gruffydd Jones was subjected to much criticism and abuse from inside the Anglican Church in Wales. In the early years it was the style of his evangelical preaching that got him into trouble, from which he was only saved by the timely intervention on his behalf by Sir John Philipps with the Bishop of St David's. Later, the criticism became deeper and more dangerous; as readers will learn in the next section of this book, the time of the circulating schools was also the time of Methodist enthusiasm in Wales, when men of the calibre of Howell Harris and Daniel Rowland, both from inside the Church of England, were advocating significant changes. Gruffydd Jones particularly fell foul of his Anglican detractors because of his friendship with John Wesley and George Whitefield.

One final thought; with all their limitations in curriculum, the circulating schools served their times well, as the Welsh people were thereby enabled to become literate, at a time when most of their English neighbours remained unable to read and write.

c. Religious

As readers will already be aware, no worthwhile account of educational activities in Wales in the eighteenth century is possible that ignores the relevance of religious factors. They will remember too that a great educational stimulus had been provided by the widespread desire to be able to read Bishop Morgan's Bible. As educational standards began to rise in the course of the century, so too the awareness of the importance of religion grew, along with the parallel awareness of the failure of many existing churches to satisfy the deep religious cravings of ordinary people.

The Church of England in Wales at this time was at an exceedingly low ebb; very little money was available, priests received utterly inadequate stipends, ignorance was widespread as was pluralism, which was inevitable in the circumstances. All these facts accumulated at a time when enlarged congregations thronged the churches, like hungry beggars clamouring to be fed. In view of these strictures, it is perhaps surprising that the Church in Wales at this time managed to produce a number of remarkable personalities of the calibre of Gruffydd Jones, Howell Harris, Daniel Rowland and William Williams of Pantycelyn, all of whom interacted on each other to a quite remarkable extent. To illustrate this interaction, it needs to be recorded that it was through listening to advice given by Gruffydd Jones that Howell Harris first started to teach, that Daniel Rowland became a changed man through hearing Gruffydd preach, just as William Williams had a similar experience through sitting at Howell Harris' feet. Again the first meeting, which was in 1737, between Daniel Rowland and Howell Harris had the most significant consequences for the future course religion was to take in Wales. However, although all these four outstanding men remained stalwart members of the Church of England, they were all subjected to much bitter vituperation from their own church leaders, and cannot therefore be regarded as belonging to the Establishment.

As well as there being a rising tide of discontent inside the Anglican church, there was also a powerful ground swell of Puritanism at work; ever since the Commonwealth had encouraged the growth and expression of dissident opinion in Wales, nonconformity had flourished, first encouraged by the unusual climate of freedom, only to be further strengthened after the Restoration of the monarchy in the fires of persecution, and finally to surge ahead after the passage of the Act of Toleration, which enabled dissident sects to worship as they pleased in their own places of worship. During these later days of expansion at the beginning of the eighteenth century, a significant educational development took place, when dissident academies were set up especially in the south-west of Wales, where future religious leaders were to be educated. Among the alumni of these academies, along with nonconformist Ministers were men like Howell Harris and William Williams, who were to change the course of religious life in their country, while still remaining in the ranks of the Anglican church. Out of the twin struggles of the emerging nonconformists and the dissatisfied Anglicans was born the Methodist movement.

Whenever the rise of Methodism in Wales is under discussion, inevitably the name of Howell Harris is the first to be mentioned. That there would eventually have been some breakaway from the Church of England seems most likely, but the actual shape of the Methodist church which finally emerged in Wales in the early years of the nineteenth century, would have been markedly different, had not Howell Harris many years before imposed his considerable powers of organisaton and his powerful personality upon the course of events.

Howell Harris' father, a joiner, was a Carmarthenshire man, who in 1700 moved to the Talgarth area of Brecknockshire in search of work; two years later he married and of the five children of the marriage, the third boy, Howell, was born in 1714. Howell's father, a humble man, was a devout Christian, who in his desire to give his son the best education possible, allowed his wife's more prosperous family to pay for his schooling at the academy at Llwyn Llwyd near Hay, in Brecknockshire. Howell stayed there until his father died three years later, when he left, equipped with enough Latin and Greek to enable him to open small schools in the district. If Howell Harris' diaries are to be taken at their face value, he was at this time something of a bad lad until Palm Sunday 1735, when at the age of twenty-one he underwent a remarkable experience in the parish church at Talgarth, where the vicar called his parishioners to repentance. This experience was to transform his life and later caused him to transform the lives of thousands of his fellow countrymen.

Without more ado Howell started to go round the district,

button-holing bystanders as he underlined the vicar's call to repentance. He stayed a teacher for three more years but after 1735 teaching was a secondary consideration. Yesterday's lay-about had become today's reformer, but his elder brother, Joseph, was less than impressed with what was happening, and, thinking to bring his young brother to his senses, pulled the necessary strings and arranged for Howell to take up a place at Oxford in the autumn. Howell however only allowed his preaching to be interrupted for a few days while he journeyed to Oxford and cancelled the arrangement before returning home and resuming his preaching. Things came to a head at Christmas, 1735, when he conducted a one-man house-to-house mission in Talgarth, calling all to repentance. From that time local opposition grew and soon hardened into confrontation. Before long the Vicar of Talgarth, whose preaching had started Howell off, clashed with him; he rebuked him and effectively stopped him from becoming an ordinand. At this moment of crisis Howell seems seriously to have considered the idea of going over to the Dissenters, but he finally and, as things turned out, permanently rejected the notion.

Meanwhile crowds flocked to hear him preach, mostly out-of-doors, presenting Howell with the problem of finding a way of keeping in touch with those he converted. This he did by organising them into small groups, which he called Societies. These early groupings around Talgarth were the first beginnings of what was to become the Methodist Movement in Wales. For the first time Howell Harris had revealed a real talent for organising.

Meanwhile readers must be introduced to another who was destined to carry the Methodist banner in Wales, Daniel Rowland, a Cardiganshire man, born in 1713, who was ordained a curate in 1735, the year of Howell Harris' conversion. Daniel Rowland also underwent a remarkable experience, in his case when he heard Gruffydd Jones preaching in the church at Llanddewi Brefi. Until 1737 the careers of the two reformers ran on parallel lines, but in 1737 Rowland heard Harris preach. The ensuing meeting was of the utmost importance for the reform movement in Wales; they were both driven by a sense of mission to bring sinners to repentance. No Welshman in the eighteenth century had a more compelling voice or a greater gift for moving a congregation than Daniel Rowland. His sermons were immensely powerful, many of his audience being held captive by his ability to frighten them almost out of their wits! He often preached away from his own parish and in unconsecrated places and in so doing incurred the gravest displeasure of the religious establishment, in consequence of which he remained a curate all his life. At this first meeting between the two men in 1737 they at once became friends, each recognising the other as a kindred spirit.

The third member of the great triumvirate of Methodist pioneers in Wales was William Williams, who was younger than Howell Harris but who was educated at the same academy. He had intended to become a doctor but one day chanced to hear Howell Harris preaching in the churchyard at Talgarth, with the immediate result that he opted to be ordained. As he became ever more evangelical he developed his musical powers and indeed became Wales' foremost writer of hymns. The eventual success of the reform movement in Wales rested firmly on the shoulders of these three remarkable men, Howell Harris, Daniel Rowland and William Williams of Pantycelyn.

From 1738, the Methodist Movement in Wales gained substantial momentum, as the partnership of Harris and Rowland began to develop and to bear fruit. By the end of that year twelve societies had been formed in Brecknockshire, four in Monmouthshire, two in Carmarthenshire, and some in Glamorgan and Montgomeryshire, all these counties having been visited and preached in by Howell Harris during the year. In the following year many adherents to the cause came to regard Harris as their leader, especially as the fourth rejection in that year of his plea for ordination gave him the freedom to preach what he liked where he liked and when he liked, whereas Daniel Rowland was at all times subject to the jurisdiction of his religious superiors.

By 1740, the Societies numbered sixty-four; with this remarkable growth members began to clamour for an acknowledged leader who would be able to exercise central control.

(At this time Harris' official title was General Superintendent). To elect such a leader the first meeting of the Welsh Calvinistic Methodist Association met in Carmarthenshire in 1742, when members had to choose between Harris and Rowland. Partisanship however became so rife that it was decided for the present to shelve making this necessary decision. Further organisation could not be shelved and at this meeting it was agreed that all Societies should hold monthly meetings, a provision being made to hold District meetings every two months and Quarterly meetings every four months. The idea of holding these tiers of meetings was certainly Howell Harris' brain child; without his skill, foresight and patience at this critical time little valuable harnessing of the Methodist Movement would have been possible. At this same meeting it was also decided not to break away from the established church, despite the protests of many dissenters who had been converted to the Methodist way of thinking.

In the 1740s the movement was at the crossroads, with both would-be leaders having fervent followings. A rift looked ominously near, especially when Harris withdrew from the leadership contest, clearly indicating that he would not be prepared to serve under Rowland. Howell continued with his preaching but frequently chose to attend Methodist meetings in London, where he became a close friend of John Wesley and George Whitefield. By 1750, Daniel Rowland was the acknowledged leader, while Harris, who had meanwhile married, and moved to Trefeca, near Talgarth, thereafter tended to distance himself from Welsh Methodists, as he became increasingly involved in something exciting that John Wesley told him he had seen at work in America from where Wesley had lately returned. Wesley's path had happened to cross that of the Moravians, whose missionaries from central Europe at this time had established socio-economic communities, where all lived, worked and prayed together. Back in Trefeca in 1752 Howell at once set about imitating the Moravians by setting up what he called the Family. A timely gift of money enabled him to start building at Trefeca straightaway; in the next few years further buildings were erected as new needs arose until, when John Wesley came to stay at Trefeca, he described what he saw as a little paradise, where a hundred and twenty people lived and worked and worshipped together. A full viable communal life was set in motion to which all members of the Family made contributions in labour and in worship. At Trefeca full scope was given to Howell Harris' genius for organisation and from small beginnings no fewer than sixty trades and crafts were practised.

In 1759, he decided that the Family was functioning so successfully that he could afford to leave it for a while; he thereupon joined the Army and saw three years of service in the Seven Years' War against France. On his return to Trefeca in 1762 he received a letter from leading Welsh Methodists, welcoming him back to Wales and expressing the hope that old quarrels might be patched up. The fact that two of the signatories were Daniel Rowland and William Williams caused Howell Harris to bury the hatchet and to resume a round of visits to Societies and Association meetings. What Harris failed to realise, however, was that in his years of isolation at Trefeca big changes had taken place in the Methodist Movement, as a result of which a new generation of impatient, able and persuasive young Methodists had arisen who had no intention of staying indefinitely inside the Church of England. However in recognition of Howell's past services they reappointed him General Superintendent.

Howell Harris died in 1773, and was buried inside the parish church at Talgarth, where thirty-eight years previously he had first seen the light; Daniel Rowland died in 1790 and William Williams the following year. With the deaths of the three great stalwarts, the old generation had passed away, its place taken by evangelistic and energetic leaders. Furthermore, whereas up to this time the south and central parts of Wales had been the centre of the Movement, Methodism now took firm root in the North where, in 1784, Thomas Charles joined the Bala Society, whose increasing influence soon made Bala the northern headquarters of Methodism. By the end of the century it was clear that the Church of England would not for much longer be a strong enough vessel to contain the spirited membership of Welsh Methodism. Independence came in 1811.

By way of postscript, readers may be interested to know that the Family at Trefeca survived for 50 years after its founder's death; in these years a printing press was established in the community, which did much to publicise Howell Harris' life and achievements. The buildings that had formerly housed the Family became a College, whose function changed over the years. Today it is a lay training centre for Welsh Methodists (the Presbyterian Church of Wales). There is also a memorial chapel to Howell Harris, adjoining which is a museum, a visit to which is recommended to all who for religious or historical reasons find the story of the second half of the eighteenth century in this part of Wales an absorbing one; to the discriminating a visit to Trefeca today, both outside and to the museum, is a wholly delightful voyage of discovery.

d. Intellectual and Imaginative

Of all the seminal events in European history none has had more importance or longer-lasting consequences than the French Revolution, which, starting as an internal quarrel in 1789 between government and people, in a few years broadened out into a European war in which the soldiers of France, as they fanned out over Europe, carried with them new ideas that thereafter were to alter the course of history in most countries of Europe in the nineteenth and further afield in the twentieth century. In short the French Revolution like the American Revolution, which preceded it by a few years, fundamentally affected the way people thought in succeeding centuries.

With the benefit of hindsight it can be seen that, after the years of terror when horrible excesses took place in the streets of Paris, certain new ideas emerged, of which the most significant were nationalism and liberalism. By the former was meant the right of people of one nationality to rule themselves, while liberalism involved the right of individuals, once national independence had been achieved, to have some say in the way in which they were to be governed.

These then were the consequences but the causes were less complicated; they were rooted in the refusal of a succession of French governments to reform their archaic systems of rigid autocracy and to limit the privileges of the minority in the interests of the down-trodden majority, a necessary change which apparently could not be brought about by constitutional means. Grievances were deep-seated and primarily economic, but, as the eighteenth century wore on, there arose men of ideas, both in France and elsewhere, including Wales, who pointed the way to fundamental change.

In fomenting the ideas that touched off revolution in America and France, three Welshmen played prominent parts, Richard Price, David Williams and Edward Williams, who preferred to be known as Iolo Morganwg. The grievances of the American colonists, which precipitated the American War of Independence in the 1770s, seem to have made a special appeal to Welshmen.

Richard Price (1723-1791), probably the foremost political thinker that Wales has produced, had been educated in several nonconformist academies in South Wales before going to London, where he became Minister of the Unitarian Church at Stoke Newington; in London he moved in intellectual circles, where he established a strong friendship with the American philosopher Benjamin Franklin, and was elected a Fellow of the Royal Society. In 1776 he wrote "Observations on the Nature of Civil Liberty", wherein he expounded the need for parliamentary reform and openly advocated the cause of the American colonist, whose war of independence had just begun.

The second Welsh supporter of revolution was David Williams, likewise a nonconformist minister until he abandoned Christianity for Deism; in 1776, in co-operation with Benjamin Franklin, he produced a Cult of Nature, which Robespierre later used as a template for his own cult of the Supreme Being. In the early years of the revolution Williams was made an honorary citizen of France, arriving in that country in 1792 and only leaving on the very day that France declared war on England. Back in London he inflamed the imagination of the third Welsh apologist of revolution, Iolo Morganwg.

In the person of Iolo Morganwg ideas and imagination met; he has at different times been regarded as scholar, poet, traveller, stone-mason, revolutionary thinker, forger and charlatan, the emphasis varying from one generation to the next. Even today it is far from easy to know where to place him in the Hall of Fame. He did make himself into a very considerable scholar, while those familiar with the Welsh language have never doubted his preeminence as a poet, but beyond any reasonable doubt he also forged many a document and foisted many an excellent poem of his own composition on to others.

Trained by his father to follow in his footsteps as a stone-mason, in 1770 he left Glamorgan for London, which in the late eighteenth century proved to be a magnet to young Welshmen, who gathered there in search of fame and fortune. There they formed associations of their fellow countrymen, of which the best known was the Honourable Society of Cymmrodorion, whose transactions to this day are of outstanding value to researchers. Iolo became a member and his rapid acquaintance with Owen Myfyr and William Owen Pughe did much to advance his literary endeavours. First however he had to establish himself as a stone-mason, which trade provided him with the necessary money and leisure to devote his spare time to further his growing reputation as a writer.

In 1777, he returned to Wales (by foot — he was a prodigious walker), and four years later married. Margaret Roberts was a truly remarkable woman; she was no wilting violet but gave as good as she got. Somehow she managed to stay loyal to her most difficult husband. In addition she had, when she married him, a good deal of money, which was to pass through her husband's fingers with almost unbelievable rapidity. Tiring of being a stone-mason, he tried to find other suitable employment, experimenting in strange ventures thanks to his wife's money. Finally funds becoming exhausted, and his debts having accumulated alarmingly, he fled from his creditors, along with his wife and three-year old daughter.

The law caught up with him; he was arrested, tried and sent as a debtor to Cardiff prison for a year. There he stayed from 1786 to 7.

To many men a fortieth birthday is something of a landmark; youth is thought past, middle age looms. Iolo might have been forgiven, had he felt downhearted, when he passed his fortieth birthday in Cardiff gaol, but in fact his year in prison turned out to be one of the most productive in his whole life. After all, his material worries were all over for the time being; his wife and child came to live near the prison, while his father, who saw to the needs of Iolo's family, frequently came to visit him. Meanwhile, Iolo, untrammelled by responsibility, spent the year reading widely and writing prose and poetry in Welsh and English; he conducted an exhaustive correspondence with a number of Welsh scholars and he learned how to play the flute. Much that he wrote in this most unusual sabbatical year was published, with the result that his reputation grew apace, while he recharged his batteries.

Above all, it was in this year that he first perfected a talent for deception; by then, thanks to his previous researches in London and elsewhere, into the poetry of Dafydd ap Gwilym, he knew a very great deal about Wales' foremost medieval poet. Armed with this knowledge, he proceeded to write many poems, in which he imitated so brilliantly the great poet's style that he was able to pass them off as genuine products of the fourteenth century poet, poems, which he claimed to have discovered in remote and unspecified locations in Glamorgan. Many of these ap Gwilym forgeries which he had made in prison, he sent to London, where they were published in a book, which Iolo edited and to which he added an appendix. The fame which resulted from the success of this book caused the author to abandon his baptismal names and proclaim himself to be Iolo Morganwg.

Fortified by a return to freedom and encouraged by the success that attended the ap Gwilym forgeries, Iolo dreamed another dream in which he planned another but different sort of deception. By 1789 he had conceived the idea of restoring Druidism to Wales, announcing his own claim to be the last surviving Druid bard. A recurring bout of restlessness, allied with the need to publicise his views on Druidism, caused him in 1791 to make a second visit to London, where before long he joined the Society of Gwyneddigion, whose membership was mostly recruited from exiles from north Wales. He found the company very congenial and stimulating, especially as much stress was laid upon the strong literary achievements of the men of Gwynedd, even going as far back as the Middle Ages.

Iolo thereafter burned with a passionate longing to do for Glamorgan what these Gwynedd members were doing for their own part of Wales. If Gwynedd had had splendid cultural traditions back in the Middle Ages, which showed themselves in many a literary reference to early eisteddfodau, then he, Iolo Morganwg, was fiercely determined to do the same for his much-loved Glamorgan, even if it became necessary to involve himself in another round of literary forgeries, which before long he produced, only to pass them off to his fellow club members as genuine manuscripts, which, according to him, he had rescued from oblivion in remote corners of Glamorgan valleys.

Iolo's obsession with Druidism was greatly increased when he discovered that there were authentic records in north Wales of long-established Druid procedures, dating from the Middle Ages, whereby poets and musicians met periodically to compete with each other in poetry and song. These were genuine traditions of medieval eisteddfodau, organised at the local level. At the end of the eighteenth century these surviving but much-diluted observances received a salutary shot in the arm by a very successful eisteddfod, which was held in Corwen in 1789 which did much to encourage future meetings.

In September 1792, Iolo made a determined effort to give his native Glamorgan at least cultural parity with Gwynedd. Earlier in the year a volume of Welsh poetry had been published to which Iolo contributed an introduction in which he stressed that contemporary Welsh poets, whose work appeared in the collection, were the true descendants of the ancient Druid bards, who had, he said, sung their songs in the valleys of Glamorgan in the Middle Ages. The publication of this book was followed by a remarkable event that took place on Primrose Hill in London on September 23rd, 1792; to that outdoor meeting Iolo had invited friends to participate in the celebration of the autumn equinox. This was the time when new styles of religious practice were being talked about, especially in France; in devising rituals and ceremonies for this occasion Iolo, though certainly influenced by current developments in France, where revolutionaries were becoming excited about nature worship, was primarily concerned with acquiring for Glamorgan a prominent place in the cultural history of Welsh bards.

The Gentlemen's Magazine in October 1792 (quoted by Stuart Piggott in *The Druids*, which is an essential source book for this subject), wrote thus.

> "This being the day on which the autumn equinox occurred, some Welsh bards resident in London, assembled in congress on Primrose Hill, according to usage. The wonted ceremonies were observed. A circle of stones formed, in the middle of which was the Maen Gorsedd, or Altar, on which a naked sword being placed, all the bards assisted to sheath it."

An accompanying chant and fervent prayers, all written by Iolo, may have caused a few eyebrows to be raised, as references to nature worship smacked at that time of David Williams and Robespierre.

By 1795, Iolo's reputation in literacy circles in London was at its peak, with the publication the previous year of his *Poems Lyrical and Pastoral*; among the subscribers listed were William Wilberforce and George Washington, a tribute to his championship of the down-trodden. It was at this time of triumph that circumstances forced him to turn his steps homewards, to take up again his long-neglected responsibilities towards his family. Valiant woman though his wife was, she could no longer cope with her problems single-handed. Iolo returned to find a state of utter destitution. Somehow a family move was arranged to Cowbridge where he had to find ways to augment the meagre sums which he was able to earn as a stone-mason. He tried his hand at a number of different jobs, which included selling books and groceries but penury was only staved off by generous gifts of money from anxious friends in London. After 1795 Iolo spent the rest of his life in Wales and, despite his preoccupation with poverty he never ceased to preach the virtues of Druidism to his fellow countrymen, stressing in particular two aspects of Druidical teaching, nature worship and belief in one god. Before the eighteenth century was out, he had also become a Unitarian, but saw no inconsistency in embracing both faiths. To those who may think Druidism and Unitarianism incompatible one can only say that in Iolo's case the common ground between the two creeds was provided by a joint acceptance of monotheism and a love of nature. He played a prominent part in setting up a Unitarian Association in south Wales (1802), for which he wrote the rules and regulations. He was also to write many Unitarian hymns, some of which are still sung in Unitarian chapels in Wales.

The even tenor of life in south Wales was rudely shattered in February 1797 by the news of the French landing in west Pembrokeshire; fine republican sentiments at once died the death as Jemima Nicholas rounded up French soldiers with her pitchfork on the cliffs above Fishguard. This indeed was no time to write poems on Liberty; instead even Iolo wrote a recruiting song for the Glamorgan Volunteers! After 1797 Iolo concentrated on preaching Druidism and Unitarianism and in helping to stimulate the general acceptance of eisteddfodau, but deteriorating health slowed him down and limited his activities, although in 1820 he did make a significant suggestion, which went unheeded for a hundred and twenty years. In proposing the formation of a Welsh Academy he was thinking not only of focusing national attention on the need to study every aspect of Welsh history and culture but also of setting up the sort of Folk Museum, which has grown since 1946 in the grounds of St Fagan's Castle, just outside Cardiff, under the expert tutelage of Iorwerth Peate.

Posterity today tends to take the view that Iolo was outstanding as an antiquary, a Welsh scholar and a poet, despite the forgeries and fabrications and the deceptions practised, for which the excuse, though not the justification must be his excessive love for all things appertaining to Glamorgan and his over-dependence on laudanum which for many years he had taken to relieve the pain of arthritis. His was one of the main influences on Welsh culture in the nineteenth century; he was a great communicator in the Welsh language, both in poetry and prose. Iolo was probably the spiritual father of Welsh nationalism and he turned the eisteddfod into a great national institution.

B
Notes and Illustrations
Iolo Morganwg — Two Anecdotes

Readers who may have become interested in the personality of Iolo may care to read of two incidents in which he was involved, the first, when he first visited London as a young man and the second many years later, when he was down on his uppers in Cowbridge; his head may have been "bloody" but most certainly had remained "unbowed"!

In his youthful desire to improve his English style he cultivated the acquaintance of a London bookseller, who told him that Dr Johnson was in the habit of visiting the shop on the first day of each month to see what new books were available. Iolo thereupon decided to waylay the great man. As soon as Dr Johnson appeared in the shop, Iolo picked up three English grammar books and, with a deep bow, introduced himself as a poor Welsh workman who wanted to improve his English, and asked him which of the three grammars he would recommend him to buy. Dr Johnson, uncouth as ever, pushed the books back at Iolo, with the ungracious throw-away comment "Either of them will do for you, young man." Iolo, much offended, answered him back with "Then, Sir, to make sure of having the best, I will buy them all" and proceeded so to do, ill though he could afford the extravagance. In time, however, he recovered sufficiently from the humiliation to boast, when consulting one of these books in company, that it was one of the books which Dr Johnson had recommended! Years later, when Iolo came to know Boswell, he told him of this snubbing, only to be informed that if only he had been patient, he would probably have come to enjoy more of the doctor's company thereafter.

Outside a shop in Cowbridge's main shopping street today will be found a wall plaque, which commemorates Iolo's brief career in later years as a shopkeeper. There he sold books, stationery and groceries, and despite little commercial success, he sometimes gladdened the hearts of residents by a certain flair for publicity. On one occasion he had on a stand in his window a book, simply entitled *Rights of Man*, which soon attracted the attention of two men, who were thought to be government agents. They entered the shop in triumph, believing the book to be Tom Paine's famous polemic. Having made the purchase, the two men realised too late that the book was none other than the Bible, causing them to call the shopkeeper a cheat and to ask for the return of their money. Iolo refused their demand with these words. "No, Sir, I am no cheat. You will find in this book the best and dearest rights of man."

Traeth Mawr

Readers may remember that early in this book reference was made to Sir John Wynn's unsuccessful attempt to involve Sir Hugh Middleton in trying to drain Traeth Mawr, which was a part of the Gwydir estates. Over the centuries other attempts were made to attempt this formidable task; indeed between 1770 and 1800 about 1500 acres were reclaimed, until 1798 a large-scale undertaking was planned under the aegis of William Alexander Madocks, who, greatly daring, tried to alter the entire landscape from the bridge at Aberglaslyn to the coast.

First he recovered sufficient land on the west of the Glaslyn estuary to build a town, Tremadog, which is worth studying as a good example of eighteenth century town-planning. From this base in Tremadog he set out to reclaim the rest of the traeth. He caused to be thrown up a great embankment, on which a road was built, to join the former west side of the Glaslyn river to the east. Completed in 1811, great praise was heaped upon Madocks and extravagant celebrations took place but before a year had passed the sea had returned and the work was entirely undone. Soon, aided by public subscription and the support of sympathisers, like the poet Shelley (who promised £100 but forgot to pay up!) and by Madocks' own fortune the nassive work was safely and satisfactorily carried out. Visitors today would do well, as they drive along the cob, or better still stand above it and look towards the hills, to venerate Madocks' memory and to reflect that this

GRUFFYDD JONES

By the time that he died in 1761, over eight thousand children had attended his schools and it is claimed that in the twenty-four years that circulating schools had existed one hundred and fifty thousand Welsh people, ranging from six years of age to seventy, had learned to read their Welsh Bibles.

CAEBACH CHAPEL, LLANDRINDOD

Situated about a mile from the centre of Llandrindod, this small, recently refurbished chapel of Caebach, built in 1715, still flies the flag of Congregationalism.

Fellow of All Soul's College, Oxford shortly afterwards died in Paris and suffered the indignity of a pauper's grave.

Thomas Pennant

There is no better contemporary picture of eighteenth century Wales and Welsh people than that afforded by Thomas Pennant's two volumes of travels in Wales in 1778 and 1781 (recently re-edited by David Kirk and to be published by Gwasg Carreg Gwalch). Pennant (1726-1798), was born near Flint and became widely respected as a traveller and historian, Dr Johnson regarding him as the best travel writer he knew. The following excerpt from the 1781 volume (*A tour in Wales*) will, it is hoped, send readers hurrying to reach for Pennant's much-neglected volumes.

> " . . . near this lake (Llyn Padarn) lived a celebrated personage . . . Margaret Evans of Penllyn . . . she is about ninety years of age . . . the greatest hunter, shooter and fisher of her time . . . she killed more foxes in one year than all the hunts do in ten . . . rowed stoutly and was queen of the lake . . . fiddled excellently and knew all our old music . . . did not neglect the mechanic arts, for she was a very good joiner and at the age of seventy was the best wrestler in the country . . . Margaret was also blacksmith, shoemaker, boat builder and maker of harps . . . she was under contract to convey the copper ore down the lakes . . . at length she gave her hand to the most effeminate of her admirers, as if predetermined to maintain the superiority which nature had bestowed on her . . . "

William Williams

It seems right that William Williams of Pantycelyn (1716-1791) should have the last word in this chapter, as scant justice was done to him in the text, where Howell Harris and Daniel Rowland stole the lime-light. Even so Williams was a travelling preacher for more than fifty years in addition to being Wales' most prolific hymn writer. His reputation too has stood the test of time, as one of his hymns is still remembered by thousands of his fellow countrymen every time the Welsh Rugby team scores a try, when one and all raise their voices to render Guide me, O Thou Great Redeemer!

THE DRUIDS ON PRIMROSE HILL 1993

Members of the Druid order (the British Circle of Universal Bond) go in procession every September to Primrose Hill in north-west London in order to celebrate the autumn equinox. This photograph, (taken in September 1993 by Chris Harris for the Times and reproduced here by kind permission of the proprietors of the Times) gives a graphic representation of Druid ceremonial. It is to be hoped that those participating realise the debt they owe to Iolo Morganwg, whose first staging of this ceremonial on Primrose Hill in September 1792 had been designed partly to give his beloved Glamorgan (Morganwg) cultural parity with Gwynedd, as the "Joneses" of south Wales tried thus to keep up with the "Joneses" of the north!

TALGARTH CHURCH

Howell Harris, who for most of his life incurred the hostility of the Established Church, was given at his death an honoured place of burial inside Talgarth church, where a tablet commemorates him. On the day of his funeral in 1773 the biggest crowd ever known to have assembled locally thronged the streets around the parish church. It was in this church, readers may care to remember, that thirty-eight years previously, on Palm Sunday 1735 Howell Harris was first moved to set in motion a train of events which finally in 1811 led a great many Welsh Methodists to break away and form an independent church.

TREFECA CHAPEL

This memorial chapel is to the memory of Howell Harris, who, born in Trefeca, not only went on to sow the seeds of Methodism in Wales but also, here in Trefeca, engineered a remarkable social experiment, a religious-industrial family community that played an important part in Welsh social history in the eighteenth century. Adjoining the chapel is a fascinating museum, which contains along with personal artefacts associated with Howell Harris rare books printed by the Trefeca Press and illuminating accounts of the activities of Harris' social experiment.

Part IV
The Industrial Revolution and Social Unrest
1800-1850

a. The Impact of the Industrial Revolution on Wales

Wales, in the eighteenth century, as it appeared in the last chapter, summoned up a picture of rural and for the most part poverty-stricken communities, small villages, where a drab and unexciting existence was periodically disturbed by the noisy arrival of the drovers, where parish priests were few and far between and where ignorance was widespread, although something worthwhile was being attempted by dedicated people to encourage and to make more meaningful the practice of religion and to provide some basic education for both young and old. There was little opportunity for most ordinary men and women to move from one part of the country to another, roads were hardly worthy of the name and transport other than that provided by the horse and Shank's pony was virtually non-existent. As the eighteenth century wore on, however, the simple agricultural economy of Wales was suddenly fractured by industrial activity, which was brought about by external circumstances.

Vital geographical discoveries, made in previous centuries, had led to the formation of trading companies overseas, which by the early years of this eighteenth century caused a great influx of raw materials into this country. The Treaty of Utrecht in 1713, marking the end of a successful war with France, gave further opportunities to increase trade outside Europe. If these new supplies of goods were to be properly utilised, industrial processes here had to be improved. Hence there was after Utrecht a conscious, deliberate attempt to change our methods of production in order to take full advantage not only of the increased supply of raw materials but also of potential export markets.

As things were, all industrial production was on a very small scale and very many industries were home-based, that is, men,

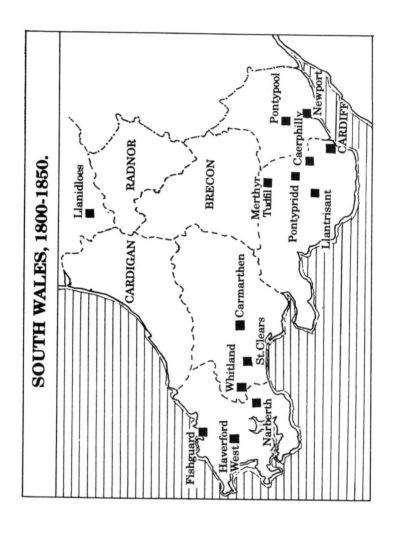

SOUTH WALES, 1800-1850.

Llanidloes

RADNOR

CARDIGAN

BRECON

Merthyr Tudfil

Pontypool

Caerphilly

Newport

CARDIFF

Pontypridd

Llantrisant

Carmarthen

St.Clears

Whitland

Narberth

Fishguard

Haverford West

women and children worked in their own homes, dealing with raw materials, supplied to them by their peripatetic employers. This was the cottage or domestic system, which enabled many families just to make ends meet, albeit often in very bad conditions and for minimal financial return. Such a system was economically unsound and could not possibly cope with the opportunities that the eighteenth century had to offer.

In Wales, from the middle of the eighteenth century, small-scale industrial activity increased and in the last twenty years of the century gained quite extraordinary momentum. In Anglesey, where Parys Mountain was found to be made of solid copper, in Neath and Swansea, where this precious copper ore was smelted by charcoal, in the slate quarries of Caernarfonshire and in the woollen mills of Llanidloes in Montgomeryshire, industrial production had been on the increase, but it is to the valleys of Glamorgan and Gwent (then known as Monmouthshire) that the attention of readers is to be directed, and above all to Merthyr Tydfil, where an immense coal-field awaited large-scale development and where even more important deposits of iron ore were about to be worked.

In 1759, the first great iron-works was set up at Dowlais, to be followed in 1765 by another at Cyfarthfa, in consequence the output of iron, smelted no longer by charcoal but by the abundant Merthyr coal, quadrupled within thirty years. Thereafter, thanks to these vast natural resources of iron and coal in the valley, Merthyr became the greatest iron and steel manufacturer in the world. By 1801 Merthyr had become the largest town in Wales and thirty years later it was found to be bigger than Cardiff, Swansea and Newport put together!

The Industrial Revolution proper really stemmed from the application of steam to industrial processes; at the same time the factory owners built as many small houses as they could to accommodate their workers in the immediate neighbourhood of their premises. These factories were unregulated, wages were low, hours of work long, working conditions downright bad, and the need for hygiene and sanitation totally disregarded. The workers' homes were overcrowded hovels, dark and damp and insanitary; perhaps the worst social evil of all was the ruthless exploitation of child labour in these places.

In the new century industry settled like a plague upon the Welsh countryside with consequences whose significance can hardly be exaggerated. In the new communities, which had been created by the development of factories and the building of workers' homes in the immediate neighbourhood, social problems speedily proliferated, as new and appalling living conditions were suffered by those employed in mills and factories and mines. Before long there began to emerge from the ranks of the workers leaders who suggested remedies for the social evils in their midst, remedies, which their employers for a very long time ignored. Then it was that the ideas of thinkers, like David Williams, whose *Right of Man* had been discredited, when the fires of revolution in France had got out of control and led to a European conflagration, were remembered in the valleys, where they quickened the understanding of the down-trodden and the dispossessed. In the social conflict, which accompanied the settling-in of the factory system, the forces of Capital and Labour crystallised, the divisions becoming the more apparent in Wales, as most of the employers there were Englishmen and most of the work force hailed from the valleys of Wales.

This then was Wales on the eve of peace in 1815, when victory at Waterloo freed the government from the exigencies of war and allowed it to turn its attention to the infinitely more taxing problems of social organisation and social justice.

b. Revolution or Reform: 1815-1831

The twenty years and more of war between France and England at the end of the eighteenth and the beginning of the nineteenth centuries acted as a powerful forcing frame for our industrial system, enabling it, with an enlarged labour force, to cope successfully with the unusually heavy demands made upon it, by the prolonged war. As far as Wales was concerned, the factory owners became very rich men, of real substance, while their employees still had to work and live in the same wholly unsatisfactory conditions that had prevailed before the war. With the coming of peace in 1815 the demand for goods suddenly fell off and an economic depression followed, which, subsequent experience has shown us, seems unavoidable after a long war. In 1815, as fewer goods were produced and wages were being reduced, Parliament, whose power base was still the land, passed a Corn Law, the effect of which was to increase the price of bread. The outlook for the working class in Wales (and of course elsewhere too in Britain), was bleak in the extreme, with conditions at home and in the factory and mine being quite unsatisfactory, with wages reduced and the price of bread put up.

In London, the Government appeared to believe that with Napoleon Bonaparte at last safely out of the way in St Helena and with the ideas of the French Revolution away in cold storage, the future would be untroubled, seemingly unaware of the plight of a great many ordinary people, whose condition on the morrow of peace was probably worse than was that of the peasants of France in 1789. The Government suffered a rude awakening in 1816, when it found its authority challenged by a riot in the capital, to which Parliament replied by passing an act to suspend Habeas Corpus, making it legal to keep a suspect in prison without bringing him to immediate trial. It was to protest against this particular instance of corking the bottle too tightly that a large number of radicals assembled in Manchester in August 1819; a peaceful and lawful demonstration turned into a shambles when the yeomanry was ordered to charge. Parliament then panicked and passed the Six Acts, one of which forbade the holding of public meetings.

To return to Wales, so straitened were the circumstances even of those in employment that most of the strikes and riots in the postwar period were organised to protest against the reduction of wages. Social grievances in those years became so intolerable that observers of the scene thought wholesale and drastic changes had to come, either by bloody revolution, as in France, or by parliamentary reform, which in the political climate after 1815 seemed most unlikely. It was a Welsh factory owner, the enlightened Robert Owen who openly expressed the opinion that a social revolution would be necessary, if the workers were to receive an adequate share of the profits of industry.

That Robert Owen was not overstating his case can be seen from the increase in the number of acts of almost barbaric violence that occurred in Wales in the 1820s. Many of these extremists, desperate men, were known as Scotch Cattle; they organised themselves into groups, who, operating in the coal and iron fields, intimidated those who opposed them. As hunger grew, so did the number of recruits for these groups. Before long the situation threatened to get out of hand. A food riot, that broke out in Nant-y-glo in 1822, speedily merged into a local war in which eventually the leaders were arrested and sent to prison. The considerable bloodshed that year can be seen in retrospect as a prelude to the greater riot in Merthyr Tydfil in 1831.

Before that ominous and momentous outbreak in Merthyr took place, there was some evidence coming out of London of a change of attitude, if not an actual sign of a move towards reform. Briefly the situation was this. Back in 1799 and 1800 Parliament, mindful of the excesses that had occurred in France, took fright and passed the Combination Acts, the effect of which was to make illegal any attempt made by workers to band together. When peace came in 1815, Francis Place, an unemployed radical, took up the cudgels on behalf of the workers but, having failed to move public opinion to take any action, in 1824, he successfully won over a Member of Parliament, Joseph Hume, who managed to persuade Parliament to repeal what after all had been a piece of war-time legislation. Ignorance and indifference rather than a change of heart probably underlay this parliamentary action, but the consequence was that from that day trade unions have at all times been legal. News of the repeal of the Combination Acts was most welcome to Welsh workers, but, perhaps surprisingly, spread dismay in the ranks of those, who had hitherto championed the workers' cause, nonconformist leaders; these men, who had for years stood up and condemned the greed of factory owners and actively supported the workers, while continuing their support, yet resolutely set their hearts against the formation of trade unions.

It was wholly appropriate that the first large scale protest against the social evils of the factory system should have taken place in Merthyr Tydfil, where all the pains of two rapid industrialisation were most keenly felt. The spark that caused the conflagration had been supplied at Cyfarthfa iron works, where the workers' wages were being reduced. The background to this protest in Merthyr however was the political upheaval that was going on in London, where the Reform Bill was being passed in the House of Commons only to be rejected by the then powerful House of Lords. In Merthyr a large political demonstration had been planned on a hill above the town where, amongst other topics, the need for parliamentary reform and the extension of the franchise were passionately debated; eventually the meeting broke up into groups, one of which, largely composed of miners and iron workers, hurried down to the town, waving their banners which called for Reform. Amid growing excitement the group raided the debtors' court, where they took possession of goods which had been confiscated by the magistrates and gave them back to their former owners. They shouted Reform but many of the rioters wanted Revolution, when units of the Argyll and Sutherland Highlanders marched to the scene, in response to an urgent summons by the frightened magistrates. The bitter fighting that followed lasted for several days before the Regular army gained the upper hand. About twenty lives were lost in the fighting, which came to an end when eighteen men were arested. These included Lewis Lewis, the chief spokesman of the men and a twenty-three year old miner, Richard Lewis, also known as Dic Penderyn, who was generally believed to have taken no part in the fighting. Strikes in sympathy were called in the valleys as the trials took place. Many of the men were convicted and transported to Australia, but the young Dic Penderyn was executed in Cardiff; in life he may at most have played only a minor role but in death he became a focal point for future dissent, contributing far more in death than he could ever have thought to achieve in life.

Three weeks later, in answer to further acts of official repression, branches of trade unions were formed in the valley, causing employers to lock out trade union members, who were forced to disband their unions, when their food supplies ran out. Nevertheless this Merthyr Riot in 1831 greatly assisted the social education of the underdogs and prepared them for even sterner encounters with authority when Chartism later became the burning issue.

c. The Spread of Unrest After 1832

Throughout the 1820s serious social unrest spread in England and Wales, as successive governments goaded malcontents to greater endeavours; in 1831, as has already been seen, a political demonstration in Merthyr Tydfil, which was aimed at furthering the cause of parliamentary reform, led to dangerous violence in the streets. Clearly Parliament, which represented only the propertied and landed classes, would have to act with unusual and uncharacteristic speed and determination if widespread trouble was to be avoided.

It was not only in the United Kingdom however that talk of revolution was in the air; in July 1830 reform had gained the victory in France, when the illiberal King Charles was replaced by a constitutional ruler, Louis Philippe. A month later the Belgians rose in revolt — and proclaimed their independence from Holland, while, another month later still, talk of the need of revolutionary change was being expressed in parts of Germany, in Poland and in Italy. Men and women in western Europe had dared to remember ideas that had been bandied about in Paris forty years before.

News of these events on the mainland of Europe further inspired would-be radical reformers at home, who came seriously to consider abandoning the quest for parliamentary reform in favour of more direct ways of achieving political change. There was a real chance of revolution here in the autumn of 1831, with angry meetings taking place up and down the country, with peasants burning hay-ricks and with workers, especially in the north, going on strike. The last chance of avoiding bloody revolution seemed to depend upon the ability of Parliament to put through really fundamental reforms.

From March 1831 to June 1832 England lived on a knife edge; in that March a bill was proposed in Parliament, which, among other provisions, abolished pocket boroughs, of which one hundred and sixty had survived. With these extra seats available new towns became parliamentary constituencies. At the same time the right to vote was given to men, living in towns, whose rent for their houses was above a certain minimum. As Parliament debated these measures, a great many people, in their excitement at the proposed changes, failed for a while to realise that, however significant and beneficial the suggested changes might prove to be, they in no way did anything to alleviate the grievances of the rapidly-increasing number of underdogs in society. When this Reform Bill painfully passed its second reading in the House of Commons — by a solitary vote, the Prime Minister resigned and called an election to give the country the chance to express approval of the bill. He succeeded in his ploy and the new parliament quickly passed the Reform Bill, but at this time it has to be remembered that for a bill to become law it had also to be accepted by the House of Lords, as well as by the Commons. In September 1831, the House of Lords did reject the bill; whereupon the House of Commons at once passed it again and again sent it back to the Lords for their decision. This impasse was overcome by the Prime Minister's acumen in asking the King to make as many new peers as would be necessary to see the bill through the Lords. The trick worked and the House of Lords, rather than see its privileges shared by newcomers, proceeded to accept the Reform Bill, which became the law of the land in June 1832.

The main achievement of this very necessary and long overdue piece of legislation was the enfranchisement of the middle class; this act may have done little to help the underprivileged, yet had done enough to fill with alarm those who were fearful of any change which might affect the status quo in society. The victor of Waterloo and former Prime Minister, the Duke of Wellington in 1832 wrote:

"The revolution is made, that is to say, that power is transferred from one section of society, the gentlemen of England, professing the faith of the Church of England, to another class of society, the shopkeepers, being dissenters from the church, and many of them atheists."

William Wordsworth, who at the fall of the Bastille forty years before, had been moved to exclaim "Bliss is it in this dawn to be alive", in 1832 talked of leaving the country "on account of the impending ruin to be apprehended from the Reform Bill."

Working class leaders meanwhile watched suspiciously as the reformed parliament set about governing the country; in their eyes the government was on probation, which they were deemed to have failed in 1834, when they tackled the problems of poverty, which were everywhere acute but nowhere worse than in the coalfields of N.E. Wales and in the newly-industrialised valleys of Glamorgan and Monmouthshire. The Poor Law Act of 1834 stated that in future no able-bodied man who lost his job would be eligible for outdoor relief. Instead the unemployed would have to live in one of the new workhouses, which the Government was to build in the wake of this act, workhouses, where they would have to work for their keep in conditions, deliberately made less attractive than those to be found in factory and mine. The working class felt itself betrayed by the middle class, many of whose members for their part disliked having to contribute in taxes for the upkeep of these workhouses.

In that same year, 1834 Robert Owen, the enlightened Welsh factory owner, formed a trade union (trade unions had been legal once the Combination Act had been repealed in 1824). His aim in setting up this Grand National Consolidated Trade Union was to encourage all workers to join for their mutual advantage. Shortly afterwards some agricultural labourers in the Dorset village of Tolpuddle, having formed a branch of Owen's union, found themselves under arrest. They were charged, not with being members of a union, but with "swearing illegal oaths", their prosecutors taking advantage of an obsolete but unrepealed act, passed in 1797 for the special purpose of dealing with a naval mutiny in wartime. The six leaders were found guilty and transported to Australia. This appalling act of official injustice, along with the rigours of the workhouses, imposed on the unemployed, together turned the workers into would-be revolutionaries.

d. The Chartists

Early Chartist agitators in England were to find eager adherents in Wales in the aftermath of the Merthyr riots of 1831; after Merthyr thoughts of reform in the workers' minds gave place to wild dreams of revolution. Fuel was added to their sense of injustice when the Reform Act of 1832 failed to give them the vote and the Poor Law Act two years later decreed that when they lost their jobs, they should go to the workhouse. Workers, with grievances such as these, along with their many middle class sympathisers, were thereafter searching for a banner under which they might enlist. The English Chartists were to supply this need. When in addition further proof of the Government's repressiveness was forthcoming in the scandalous treatment meted out to the Tolpuddle labourers who had dared to form a trade union branch (ten years after Parliament had made trade unions legal!) a great many men in England and Wales — and not all of them members of the working class — decided to nail their colours to the mast.

In 1836 some London artisans, led by William Lovett, formed the London Working Men's Association and proceeded to draw up a charter of their aims and aspirations. Similar associations were formed in other towns in the Midlands and in the North, which in a year or two combined to form a national association. So very critical were many contemporary reports of these so-called revolutionaries that it would be as well to find out what their charter consisted of. To begin with, every man should have the vote; and parliament should be elected every year, the voting to which should be in secret. Constituencies should contain an equal number of voters, while members of Parliament should be paid. Finally men should no longer have to own property in order to qualify to stand as candidates for Parliament. Such demands were reasonable, if Utopian in the political climate of the 1830s. The methods however advocated in different parts of the country differed very widely. In some parts the Chartists preferred a moderate, constitutional approach, while elsewhere, as in those parts of Wales, where social grievances were at their most bitter, violent solutions were frequently sought. The Chartist movement, it has to be said, suffered greatly in the public mind from this disparity of methods advocated. The first Chartist group to be formed in Wales was at Carmarthen, its champion none other than the middle class lawyer, Hugh Williams, of whom more will be said when the Rebecca Riots are under consideration. In general Welsh nonconformity was on the side of the Chartists, not, of course, because they agreed with violent methods, but rather because the avowed aims of the Chartists were held to be in accordance with Christian principles.

The critical year for the Chartists in Wales was 1839, when a bitter riot broke out in Llanidloes, a small but important wool-weaving town in Montgomeryshire, only to be followed later in the year by a tragic farce in Newport. 1839 was also the year, readers will discover in the next chapter, in which Rebecca and her daughters first gave public expression to their pentup rage.

As prelude to what was to come in Llanidloes, it has to be noted that a few months before the rioting began, Henry Hetherington, the national Treasurer of the London Working Men's Association, had paid the town a visit. News of this official Chartist interest in the plight of the distant wool-weavers in Llanidloes caused some alarm in official quarters, where the Government, already alerted to the intended march of Chartists to London, planned to send a squad of London policemen to Llanidloes to reinforce the local forces of law and order. Arrangements were also made to hold military forces at readiness, to be drafted into central Wales, in the event of civil unrest taking place. Certainly the wool-weavers of Llanidloes lived and worked in such deplorable conditions and for such low wages that their poverty was thought to be far the worst of any industrial district in the whole of Wales. With tension high both in the ranks of the magistrates and of the workers one small incident was sufficient to touch off a very ugly riot. One day in April a London constable, lately arrived in the town, saw fit to arrest a wool-weaver, who was walking through the town on the way to his vegetable garden with a garden spade over his shoulder. From such seemingly trivial incidents are riots made. Furious fellow wool-weavers, alerted and alarmed by this stupid act of arrogant officialdom, took immediate retribution when they imprisoned three of the London policemen in the Trewythen Arms Hotel. The magistrates thereupon called in the soldiery and five days of intermittent skirmishing followed between the rioting wool-weavers and units of the militia, by whom authority was eventually restored. Of the forty wool-weavers arrested thirty-two were to find themselves on trial at the next Montgomeryshire Assizes, their offence "drilling and marching in unauthorised groups", their punishment transportation to the other side of the world, from which fate not even the freely-given services of the lawyer, Hugh Williams, were able to save them.

Meanwhile in England the Chartist plan to march peacefully to London where they wanted to present their charter and an accompanying petition to Parliament, finally came to fruition in July 1839, when a petition, bearing more than a million signatures, was duly carried into the House of Commons, where the charter was debated and rejected. This setback tended to encourage the more extreme elements in the movement, especially in Wales, where the anger and resentment that followed the harsh punishment received by the Llanidloes Chartists, helped to swell the number of recruits to the Chartist ranks. Momentum was added, by the failure of peaceful protest in London, to the plan in south Wales to adopt more violent policies in the autumn of that year. Preparations were soon in hand to organise and to arm a military-style march down the valleys to Newport; the capture of Newport by the Chartists was intended to be followed up with a further attack on Monmouth, with the avowed object of freeing from prison Henry Vincent, who was the Chartist movement's most successful orator.

As summer gave place to autumn in 1839, all the talk in the well-patronised public houses in the valleys north and north-west of Newport was of the forthcoming march. Many people must have known about the coming "secret" march, as conspirators foregathered in local public-houses, especially in Blackwood, Blaina and Bryn-mawr, in Nant-y-glo, Pontypool and Tredegar. The acknowledged leader of this Chartist enterprise was John Frost, a former magistrate and mayor of Newport, who organised the march, the basic idea of which caught the Welsh imagination; many passed under John Frost's spell, including men as eccentric and as different as Zephaniah Williams, who was a publican, and William Price from Pont-y-pridd, a fiery and unorthodox general practitioner, who had for the time being switched his interest in Druidism to Chartism. He began to assume a dominant place in the movement, after making a long and eloquent appeal in Welsh to an enthusiastic public meeting in Blackwood. The contribution he was called upon to make to the common armoury, hidden away in the caves above the valley, was "seven pieces of cannon". In the event Price took no active part in the march, but more will be written about this truly remarkable character in the Notes that follow this chapter, where there will also be more information about the later life of John Frost.

In all, several thousand men were drilled and armed and mobilised for the Newport march; most of them came from the coal-mines and the iron works. They were organised into three parties, which were to march separately towards Newport, the eastern column under William Jones of Pontypool, the central one led by Zephaniah Williams, the other in the west under the command of the leader, John Frost. The overall plan was for the three columns to meet at the agreed time at the Welsh Oak public-house, in the outskirts of Newport, from where a unified attack would be mounted against the town. The arms carried by the marchers ranged from billhooks and pikes to swords and old guns. When they left their points of muster on November 4th, the weather was already wild and windy but in the course of the day the conditions became appalling. The nearer the three parties drew to

Newport, the more dishevelled and the less disciplined they became, with many men much the worse for drink. All the same Frost's party met Williams' party at the Welsh Oak, though William Jones and his men never made the rendezvous. Next morning, November 5th, Frost led the leading party of several hundred men into Newport, where they found it ominously quiet everywhere, with the streets quite empty and the windows of the houses carefully shuttered against any attack. Frost halted his men in the middle of the town, outside the Westgate Hotel, which the Mayor had made his headquarters, at his side thirty soldiers and some special constables. A solitary shot rang out before Chartist hatchets broke down the front door, allowing Frost's men to burst into the hotel where hand-to-hand fighting ensued, while other soldiers from the open windows of the hotel fired their muskets at those Chartists who were standing about outside. It was all over in a quarter of an hour, the hapless attackers escaping as best they could along side-streets before seeking the security of the hills. The bodies of the dead were laid out in the square, which sympathetic citizens in after years renamed John Frost Square. Many failed to make good their escape and were arrested. At the next Monmouthsire Assizes, eight leaders, including John Frost, were sentenced to death, all of them subsequently reprieved and sent to Australia for life. The march was a fiasco and a humiliating failure; the conspirators went back home, with their heads bowed; their bitter grievances, unresolved, were left to fester.

Three years later the Chartists tried for a second time to interest the Government in their Charter, and for a second time they failed. A general strike was then called, but nothing came of it except a marked increase in official repression, which resulted in fifteen hundred arrests being made. Of that number seventy-nine were transported to Australia. In 1843, the flame of Chartism briefly flickered for the last time in Wales, when a secret branch was established in Merthyr Tydfil, whose members agreed to make weekly contributions to help in the purchase of a cache of firearms. Chartism might thereafter have been expected gradually to have faded from view, but for a general tendency in Europe in the 1840s among the intelligentsia who had survived repression to think once again in terms of revolution.

Hence in London the Chartists for the third and last time in 1848, that brave year of revolutions, once more, produced the Charter, accompanied by a petition of mammoth proportions, but public opinion seemed no longer to be interested. The Government rejected it with contempt, this time not even deeming it necessary to make any arrests. This indeed seemed to be the very end of Chartism. In the short view this may have been true, as Chartism had been defeated by a revival in trade and by a start being made in vital social reform. If a longer view be taken however it will appear that the Chartists had succeeded, by their repeated willingness to agitate, in bringing forward the time when certain important changes would be made, such as the repeal of the Corn Laws and the passing through Parliament of acts, which began to regulate conditions in the mines and began to make the government responsible for public health. Politically the Chartists did fail to achieve their aim of getting the working man the right to vote. On the other hand five of the six demands in their charter (all save the annual calling of parliament) passed into law after the 1860s, when the Liberal party, who represented the middle class, made these demands a part of their own policy.

By the middle of the nineteenth century, despite the seeming failure of Chartism, the ordinary man, in England and in Wales, was slowly fighting his way to the surface. He was coming of age, even though he did not get the right to vote until 1867, if he lived in a town, or later still until 1884, if he worked on the land.

e. Rural Unrest and the Rebecca Riots 1839-43

The rioting associated with the Rebecca movement and the Chartists went on at the same time, both providing outlets for the expression of social grievances; indeed in Wales men like Hugh Williams were engaged in both activities. Nevertheless in two important respects there were real differences between the two uprisings; to start with, the Rebecca riots were confined to Wales, and to a relatively small part of Wales, while the Chartists were openly militant in industrial areas both in England and in Wales. The other difference is far more significant, in that, while Chartism was a working class activity, the Rebecca movement was very much a middle class affair, although it is true that over the years many farm labourers certainly enrolled under the Rebecca banner. Hugh Williams, who was a great driving force, was a solicitor, and he received much help and encouragement from others with a similar social status to his own, like magistrates and nonconformist ministers. The bulk of the followers of Rebecca however were farmers and tenant farmers, men who, as will be seen, suffered much from the imposition of tolls on the turnpike roads; they were also members of a class who much resented having to pay in their taxes for the upkeep of workhouses which the 1834 Poor Law caused to be built.

Agriculture in Wales had not experienced the benefits which an agricultural revolution had brought to some parts of England; an economic depression in the twenties and the thirties had produced general unrest in rural areas at a time when there was an influx of population, the effect of which was a serious food shortage. Poverty in Wales was everywhere rife. In addition the land was of poor quality and depended upon frequent applications of lime to make it produce reasonable crops. Since the middle of the eighteenth century many lime-kilns had been built, mainly in coastal areas, to which the farmers brought their carts to collect the essential lime, travelling along new roads which the turnpike trusts had built from the coasts up into the hills. Herein was to lie the most obvious grievance felt by the farming community. On average a farmer had to pay up to three shillings for a load of lime, when he collected it from the kiln, but on the journey the tolls imposed at the various toll-gates were on average double that amount. Glaring injustice though the imposition of such tolls may seem to be, the existence of these toll-gates should not be held to be solely responsible for the ensuing riots. The gates acted as visible reminders of their grievances; the real cause of the riots was the poverty, which seemed as real to the middle as it did to the working class.

The Rebecca movement was uniquely Welsh; it made a great appeal to Welsh imaginativeness and it was wrapped in mysterious secrecy, so much so that to this day not all its secrets have been divulged and no one knows for certain the identity of the leader, even though the finger of probability is pointed at Hugh Williams, about whom more will be told in the next chapter. Protected by a passionately loyal countryside these would-be leaders of rural insurrection elected one of their number as leader to whom the soubriquet of Rebecca was given. Many of the conspirators were probably nonconformists and all, who could read, were very familiar with the Bible, where in chapter twenty-four of Genesis an account is given of how Abraham chose Rebecca as a suitable wife for Isaac; her family, greatly approving of Rebecca's selection, said, in verse sixty, "Thou art our sister, be thou the mother of thousands and millions and let thy seed possess the gate of those who hate them." Before long reports were being circulated of the so-called daughters of Rebecca, riding on horseback with blackened faces in the midnight hour, all of them male, though many of them wore female attire; thus arrayed they struck terror into the hearts of those whose job it was to hold the toll-gates on the turnpike roads.

The Rebecca Riots began in earnest in 1842, but a preliminary skirmish in 1839 proved to be a useful rehearsal for the daughters of Rebecca. In January 1839 the trustees of the Carmarthenshire Turnpike Trust at Whitland decided to erect four extra toll-gates on important lime-carrying roads from a lime kiln south of Narberth up into the hills to the north and north-east of the town. Early in May two of these gates were in place at Efail-Wen and at Maesgwyn. Tension had been rising for some time in west Wales; indeed there had even been an attempt in January to set fire to the newly built workhouse in Narberth, and in April, the fires of resentment were further fuelled by news of what was happening up in Llanidloes.

The daughters of Rebecca went into action for the first time in May, when they destroyed the week-old toll-gate at Efail-wen (and went on to burn down the toll-house too). A week later a new gate was in position, which was duly destroyed early in June. Soon the new gate at Maes-gwyn was attacked and put out of action. A challenge had been thrown down to the powers-that-be, which was answered by the despatch from Brecon of a squad of soldiers to keep the peace. At the end of July the local magistrates decided that there was no real need for the four extra gates, which had been sanctioned in January. With the revoking of this order peace was restored to the district. The first round had been won by Rebecca. Thereafter there were no more attacks on toll-gates for three and a half years until the winter months of 1842, when real trouble began.

Despite a more than satisfactory harvest, which followed a hot, dry summer, social stresses apparently could no longer be contained; a new gate erected near St Clears gave the signal for the renewal of Rebecca hostilities, and on a more ferocious scale than before. The gate at St Clears was at once destroyed, and as speedily rebuilt before the daughters of Rebecca destroyed it for the second time, and for good measure went on to destroy another gate the same night. To cope with this emergency special constables were enrolled but all to no avail as they received individual warnings from Rebecca about what would happen to them if they were to do their duty. Marines were then brought in from Pembroke Dock. Meanwhile gates were being attacked as far away as on turnpike roads around Haverfordwest and Fishguard. Readers who would like to read a full and authoritative account of the tumultuous events of 1842 and 1843 are recommended to read David Williams' book *The Rebecca Riots*. Many rioters were arrested and many received savage sentences, but still Rebecca rode. As summer lapsed into autumn, reports came in of serious clashes west of Carmarthen.

The final sequence of events was played out far away from west Wales, when in the following autumn, 1843 Rebecca rode for the last time, into the remote regions of north Radnorshire, where the six approach roads into Rhayader were equipped with six toll-gates. Here the daughters of Rebecca set out on a campaign to clear the toll-gates from the roads; after some initial successful skirmishing the climax to the campaign came early in November, when fifty Rebecca rioters, armed and on foot, marched in three separate parties into the middle of the town, where they joined forces and together destroyed a gate, before marching on with military precision to four other gates, which they in turn burned down, despite the efforts made to stop them by a metropolitan police sergeant, sent down from London, at the head of a squad of special constables. A month later the remaining operational gate was similarly treated but this action proved to be the very last instance of Rebecca violence. The Rebecca riots were suddenly over.

At the time when the Rebecca riots in Rhayader had started, Government in London, at last listening to the advice that reached their ears from various sources in Wales and in particular taking notice of suggestions put to them by the sympathetic Times correspondent in Wales, set up a Commission of Enquiry, which started its work in the autumn in Carmarthen, where it took evidence from all interested parties; this peripatetic commission, which spent 35 days actually conducting interviews in all the trouble spots, finished its work, — in Rhayader. In March 1844, the Commission presented its report to Parliament, which acted with commendable speed in passing an act which became law in August, whereby in general terms the whole system of toll-gates and turnpike roads was overhauled and reformed. In so doing the main demands of the daughters of Rebecca were met; as they disbanded their forces, they were able to claim a very considerable victory. The long struggle, brutal as it had sometimes become, seemed to have served its purpose.

Full justice to the Rebecca movement will not have been done however if only its practical success in getting the turnpike and toll-gate system reformed is highlighted; the secrecy, which attended all its activities, may have prevented some of their other efforts from receiving much publicity. Suffice it to say that some of the leaders of the movement constituted themselves into an unofficial but effectual Watch Committee, which threatened with dire punishment certain named individuals who had fathered illegitimate children without making adequate provision for the upbringing of their off-spring, while other well-established members of society, who were known to have maltreated their wives, were left in no doubt about the consequences if they continued with their cruelty.

In addition to the success enjoyed by the daughters of Rebecca in alleviating a particular grievance, one other fact needs to be stressed for the part it played in relieving social pressures in the countryside of west Wales at this time, and that is the swift development in the middle of the century of the railway system up the valleys, which provided an invaluable safety-valve for the over-populated rural areas, whose unemployed were thus able to find jobs in the rapidly expanding industries down below.

f. Wales in Mid-century

The last five sections have concentrated on the problems and growing grievances of those Welshmen who lived and worked in the coal and iron fields of north-east Wales and in the newly-industrialised valleys of the south and west, along with their agricultural hinterland. Little has been said about the rest of the country, where life was being lived at a less demanding speed, although here too the yeast was beginning to rise. The census figures for 1801 and 1851 tell a truly remarkable story, as between those two dates the population of Wales doubled. Whereas at the beginning of the nineteenth century most people claimed, however tenuously, an association with the Church of England, by mid-century an astonishing change had come about, as in the 1851 census eighty per cent of the population admitted to being nonconformist. In 1801, the Baptists and Independents (Congregationalists) had been the torch-bearers of nonconformity, with the Unitarians beginning to catch up, but ten years later Welsh Methodists at long last declared themselves free of the Established Church, and started a separate independent existence. In the following four decades so successful did these spiritual descendants of Howell Harris become that by 1851 they had supplanted the Baptists as the Nonconformist church with the greatest number of adherents. By this time the Nonconformist churches were producing outstandingly able leaders in public life, men of the calibre of Henry Richard and Samuel Roberts. Meanwhile, while Congregationalists of this quality were spearheading social reform movements, at the grass-roots level up and down the country Methodist ministers were taking upon their shoulders the burdens of the people they served, identifying with the hardship and the social injustice suffered at this time by so many men and women.

As the next great landmark in Welsh history is strictly speaking beyond the terms of reference of this book, only a passing comment will be made here about the General Election of 1868, when the working class of Wales, enfranchised the previous year, helped to elect twenty-one Liberal Members of Parliament, perhaps the most distinguished of whom was Henry Richard, who was to represent Merthyr Tydfil for the next twenty years.

B
Notes and Illustrations

It is perhaps not altogether surprising that so dramatic a period of Welsh history as the Chartist agitation should have thrown up such dramatic characters as Hugh Williams, John Frost and William Price. The indulgence of readers is sought for this addendum, which is being made use of solely for the purpose of drawing attention to these eccentric contributors to the story of Wales.

Hugh Williams

Mention has already been made of the part Hugh Williams played in the Chartist agitation of Wales and of his deep involvement in the Rebecca movement, of which in all probability he was the actual leader. Hugh was born in Machynlleth in 1796, of middle class parentage; he qualified as a solicitor and practised in Carmarthen, where he married a woman twenty-five years older than himself, a woman of great wealth and property. His younger brother, who was also a solicitor, practising in London, invited Hugh to the capital, where he was introduced to the leaders of the London Working Men's Association, whose treasurer, Henry Hetherington, became a firm friend. Through Hugh's influence Hetherington visited Wales, where he vigorously campaigned on behalf of the Chartist cause; readers may remember that Hugh Williams unsuccessfully defended the Llanidloes wool-weavers after their abortive riot in 1839. Apart from his leadership of the Rebecca movement, where he displayed remarkable powers of oratory in pleading the cause, he also took an active part in the Anti-Corn Law League, of which the leading figure was Richard Cobden, who had married Hugh's sister. Cobden's children were often known to refer to their mother's brother as "wicked Uncle Hugh"! His philandering was well-known!

In 1851, the excitement of Rebecca and Chartism well behind him, he was made Recorder of St Clears, where ten years later, in 1861 his wife died, aged 90. Two months later Hugh remarried, his

By Her Majesty's Command,
£100 REWARD

WHEREAS LEWIS HUMPHREYS, late of Llanidloes, Shoemaker, and THOMAS JERMAN, of the same place, Carpenter, were apprehended at Llanidloes on the 30th of April last, on a charge of Felony, and rescued by a Mob, and have since absconded;

THIS IS TO GIVE NOTICE,
That the above Reward of

One Hundred
POUNDS

will be paid to any Person who will reapprehend, or give such information as will lead to the re-apprehension, of the above-mentioned Persons; and that

FIFTY POUNDS

will be paid to any one who will reapprehend, or give such information as will lead to the reapprehension, of either of the said two Persons.

The said Lewis Humphreys (called *John*) is a Shoemaker, about 30 years of age, 5 feet 10 inches high, of dark forbidding countenance, muscular, high cheek bones and shoulders, has dark hair, black whiskers, and probably wears a blue coat, striped trowsers, and cap.

The said Thomas Jerman is a Carpenter, aged about 30, stands about 5 feet 8 inches high, stoutly made, has broad round shoulders and short thick neck, a round wide face, small eyes, and wide mouth; when last seen, had on a blue or brown coat, light-yellow cotton waistcoat with a sprig pattern upon it, white trowsers with stripes on it, and light-striped cotton neckerchief. The fingers of his right hand are slightly contracted, and the third and fourth fingers of his left hand are much contracted.—*Both are natives of Llanidloes.*

The Reward above mentioned will be paid by the MAYOR OF LLANIDLOES, who is authorized by Her Majesty's SECRETARY OF STATE to offer the same.

JONES, PRINTER, LLANIDLOES.

PUBLIC POSTER IN LLANIDLOES, 1839

As readers will see, two local men, arrested in the Chartist uprising in Llanidloes in April 1839, had been rescued by their friends. This poster provides a clear and revealing commentary on events in Llanidloes in that ugly Spring of 1839. Lewis Humphreys and Thomas Jerman have received posthumous recognition they can hardly have envisaged.

second wife this time his junior and by thirty-nine years! They moved to Ferryside, where Hugh died in 1874, aged seventy-seven, the proud father of four children by his second wife.

John Frost

Of the Chartists, convicted after the abortive attack on Newport and sentenced to transportation to the far side of the world, most died in captivity, but their leader, their General, whose beliefs had caused him to abandon his successful career as a draper, a magistrate and a mayor, was eventually pardoned after serving fourteen years in Tasmania. In 1854 he came home to Newport, where he was welcomed by former Chartist sympathisers, who had come to the station in a horse-drawn cart, suitably decorated with flowers. Stalwarts among them took out the horses from the shafts, and then donned the harness themselves and proceeded to pull the triumphant hero, now seventy years of age, through the streets of the town. John Frost died more than twenty-three years later, at the ripe age of 93 in 1877.

William Price

Of the charismatic characters already described Hugh Williams supplied the leadership and the oratory, and John Frost the idealism but the third man, William Price was quite different, as he was certainly no leader and no orator, though he did sometimes speak persuasively in public, mostly in courts of law, while it would stretch credulity too far to call him an idealist, rather than a crank. A strong case may however be made for regarding him as the outstanding Welsh eccentric of the nineteenth century as well as being in his own odd way, a very good friend to the under-privileged and the downtrodden. William Price was a doctor, both physician and surgeon, who practised at various times in his very long career at Caerphilly, Pontypridd, Treforest, Nantgarw and at Llantrisant, where in 1893 he died, aged ninety-three.

The physical appearance of this most striking of anti-

MARKET HALL, LLANIDLOES

This beautiful timbered market hall, which was built in 1609, was at the very centre of the Chartist uprising in 1839. Over the centuries the open lower part has provided shelter for the market stalls, while up above the local council met. Here also was the home of the local museum, which has in its guardianship a priceless collection of historical objects, including much invaluable contemporary evidence of the Chartist troubles. An attempt to get this market hall taken down in the 1930s in order to speed up traffic was frustrated by public opinion but in 1994 more stringent regulations caused the museum to be temporarily closed while a new home was prepared. The newly-sited museum opened its doors in August 1994.

establishment figures, whose patients were mostly miners and farm labourers, matched the strangeness of his way of life. He was a man of above average height, with a very prominent nose and fierce, staring eyes; his beard was long, as were the black plaits of hair at the back of his head. In his dress he favoured red, white and green; over a white tunic, which he was reputed to change every day, he wore a striking red jerkin, his trousers were of some green material and over his head of black hair he often wore the skin of a fox, whose paws lay on his forehead, as its brush dangled down his back between his plaits.

His views on hygiene were quite modern, even though their application was often extraordinary; for instance he was so obsessed with cleanliness that he always refused to wear any socks, despite the fact that he was in the habit of walking great distances and always visited his patients, many of whom lived many a mile up the valley, on foot. Further evidence of this trait is furnished by his absolute insistence on washing all coins, handed over to him as fees, before making sure that he also washed his own hands. It is perhaps not surprising that he was also a vegetarian, though his reasoning was unusual, as he believed that animal passions might possess those who ate animal flesh! He never owned a watch, claiming that a good doctor had no need to know the time but called upon his patients when they sent for him. In addition he preferred to make his visits at night because he believed that his patients had greater need of him then, as sick people generally felt worse at night. He had no time at all for man-made institutions, whether they were churches or courts of law. He was at loggerheads with the law all through his life, while he made no secret of his aversion to all churches and, above all, chapels. Marriage he utterly rejected, preferring the pleasures that free love dispensed.

During the 1820s and 30s, Dr Price spent much of his leisure time acquainting himself with early religions, as a result of which he became fascinated by everything to do with the Druids. As he became more and more involved in Druid affairs, he managed to convince himself that he was descended from ancient Druids and indeed in time he went on to claim to be an archdruid. As he

CHARTIST ATTACK ON NEWPORT

This is a contemporary artist's impression of the Chartist attack, led by John Frost, on the Westgate Hotel, the seat of authority on a bleak and wet November morning in 1839.

A CONVICT SHIP

Typical of the kind of transport provided by the government of the day to convey to the other side of the world those convicted of participating in the Chartist and Rebecca uprisings.

became disappointed with the lukewarm interest local residents took in his Druidism, he became fired with enthusiasm for something else, which had a similar appeal for him. He had for some time nursed a yearning for republicanism, which the political conditions of the 1830s tended to encourage; this new political awareness he now felt the need to inculcate in others. The stark social stresses of the time affected the lives of a great many Welshmen in the valleys. With Chartist developments in south Wales he was in complete sympathy, Chartism becoming for him a more than worthwhile additional interest to Druidism. As he healed the sick he talked about Chartism and succeeded thereby in winning many converts among his patients. In after-years Price defended his absence from the march on Newport by disclosing that at the eleventh hour he had been warned not to participate as the soldiers had been given specific orders to shoot the "one with the long hair". True or false, he regarded discretion as the better part of valour and went underground. Despite his absence from the ranks of insurrection, Price thought it wise to stay in hiding, as a warrant had been issued for his arrest. Soon he shaved off his beard and disguised himself as a woman, his long plaited hair coming to his assistance. At the dockside in Cardiff he was helped up the gangway of a coastal ship, bound for Liverpool, by the police inspector, who had been sent to the docks to arrest the wanted man! The sea journey was interrupted by a forty-eight hour stop in Milford Haven, where William Price made a short call on shore, from which he returned to the ship with considerable speed, when someone penetrated his disguise. The rest of the journey was uneventful and, after disembarking at Liverpool, he took a train to London, where he rejoiced to see, pinned to a post, the offer of a reward of £100 for his capture, dead or alive! He then crossed to France, where he stayed until the following summer, when, believing that all danger was past, he quietly went home to Wales.

Soon he was able to ease himself back into his practice but he soon gave proof that he had no intention of changing his opinions. Apparently he formed the habit of holding Chartist meetings in his own home on Sunday afternoons, but the attendance never

REBECCA IN ACTION
An artist's impression of a ferocious "female" attack on a toll-gate.

exceeded thirty and, according to local gossip more time was spent in talking about Druidism than about Chartism. Nevertheless he became on his daily sick visits more and more concerned about the miners' grievances and did all he could to publicise their misfortune; whenever they went on strike, he openly identified with them, frequently speaking up at their meetings on behalf of his patients and friends.

However his greatest collision with the law still lay many years ahead of him in extreme old age, but as this contest did not take place until 1884 no detailed account can possibly be justified here; it may well be that the appetites of some readers may be whetted to find out more when they learn that in that year William Price succeeded in getting cremation legalised in the most bizarre circumstances. Nature tends to break the mould in which a Dr Price was cast!

Those who would like to know more about William Price are recommended on their next visit to the superb folk museum at St Fagans, just west of Cardiff, to investigate the medicine section of the Gallery of Material Culture, where objects relating to William Price's medical practice are on view. Then, if time allows, a further visit is suggested, to Llantrisant, about four miles north-west of St Fagans, where in the Bull Ring may be seen a life-sized bronze statue, whose inscription reads:

Dr William Price--(1800-1893). Surgeon, Chartist,
Self-styled Druid.

HUGH WILLIAMS

Hugh Williams, one of the most outstanding Welshmen of the nineteenth century, played leading parts in both the Chartist and the Rebecca protests; in the former as well as assuming a vital rôle as agitator, he also, as a man of law, defended Chartist prisoners, while in the contemporary Rebecca movement, he may well have been "Rebecca", although even to this day secrecy still surrounds the leader's identity. Idealist, man of action, lawyer and conspirator Hugh Williams lived long enough to dispense justice as the Recorder of St Clears.

HENRY RICHARD

Henry Richard was born in 1812 in Tregaron, where a statue to his memory stands in the main square opposite the Talbot Arms, where the drovers stayed before setting out on their arduous trek eastwards over the Cambrian Mountains. Richard became a Congregationalist minister with a growing interest in international peace, earning him the nickname of "The apostle of Peace". M.P. for Merthyr from 1868 until his death in 1888, his main claim to fame in those years was his successful lobbying for an act of Parliament to ensure secret voting at elections. Thanks, above all, to him, the Ballot Act became law in 1872.

JOHN FROST

In 1839 John Frost was fifty-five years old, respectable, respected, a shopkeeper, a former Mayor of Newport and still a Justice of the Peace; all this he threw away to take charge of the Chartist army, which planned to capture Newport. Military failure was followed by arrest, trial, and a death sentence which was commuted to transportation to Tasmania. In 1854, John Frost, at 70, was pardoned and brought back to Newport, where he was to spend the last twenty-three years of his life, once again an honoured citizen. No work of fiction could provide a less credible plot!

DR WILLIAM PRICE

Llantrisant's last tribute to her famous citizen came in 1982, when this bronze statue was unveiled one May morning in the presence of a large crowd, which had gathered to witness the ceremony and to join in the singing of a song, specially written for the occasion, and sung to the tune of GOD BLESS THE PRINCE OF WALES!

List of Maps and Illustrations

Maps

Illustrations

Index of Place-names

ACKNOWLEDGEMENTS

The following are the owners of the copyright of illustrations and have kindly permitted their use.

NATIONAL MONUMENT RECORDS OF WALES
(on pages 32, 75, 79, 117 and 118)

WALES TOURIST BOARD
(on pages 34, 37, 67 and 144)

THE PROPRIETORS OF THE TIMES NEWSPAPERS LIMITED
(page 116 (photograph by CHARLES HARRIS)

NATIONAL TRUST
(page 39 — the copyright of PAUL KAY)

THE RADNORSHIRE MUSEUM
(page 142)

NEWPORT MUSEUM AND ART GALLERY
(page 151)

MIKE RUDKIN, MICHAEL BERNARD PHOTOGRAPHY, LLANTRISANT
(page 152)

GWASG CARREG GWALCH
(page 41)

NATIONAL LIBRARY OF WALES
(page 151)

WALES BEFORE 1066 — A GUIDE
by Donald Gregory

144 pages; 4 maps, many illustrations; ISBN: 0-86381-117-5; Price: £3.00

Wales is a land full of the remains of its long and colourful history. Not always, however, do these ancient monuments yield themselves easily to the casual visitor. This book guides us to these historical locations to see standing stones, cromlechs, old churches, Roman remains, ancient wells and Celtic crosses. It gives a brief history of the periods before 1066 and detailed directions to these out-of-the-way spots.

The author is a retired historian who lives in Shropshire.

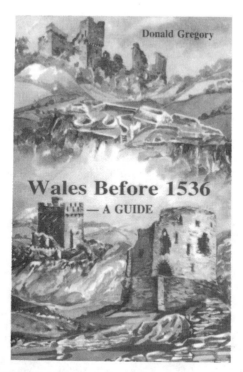

WALES BEFORE 1536 — A GUIDE
by Donald Gregory

160 pages; black & white illustrations & maps; £4.50; ISBN: 0-86381-250-3

Wales Before 1536, a companion volume to *Wales Before 1066*, continues the story of Wales, as the struggle deepened not only between the Welsh and the Saxons and the Vikings, but also between the various jealous warring Celtic power bases in north, central and south Wales. By the time this wasteful internal bickering began to give place to a strong determination on the part of most Welsh people to unify their county, power east of Offa's Dyke had passed from the Saxons to the Normans, who were far better equipped than their predecessors had been to destroy the Welsh dream of independence.

Wales provides a treasure-house of the past and with the help of this book, readers may visit the historic sites mentioned in the text. But appreciating a country's inheritance is more than looking at castles, monuments and abbeys. Hopefully, the pleasure of your search into the past will reveal the richness of this nation's identity.

Radnorshire: a Historical Guide
by Donald Gregory
Price: £4.50; many maps and illustrations; 168 pages; ISBN: 0-86381-284-8.

Radnorshire in many respects is Wales in microcosm — hilly, wild, beautiful and small. It has prehistoric settlements, very early Christian llans, ruins of medieval castles and sites of former battles. Later, nonconformists spread their ideas and built their chapels and the drovers crossed the hills with their flocks until the railway came to usher in modern times. But the past is ever-present in this old county which lends its wealth to this highly readable guide.

COUNTRY CHURCHYARDS IN WALES
by Donald Gregory

176 pages; many illustrations & maps; £3.50; ISBN: 0-86381-183-3

Cock-fighting and Celtic crosses; dancing and sun-dials; prehistoric sites and the burial grounds of Welsh princes; games and lych gates; potent drinks and strange epitaphs — these are a few of the interesting things drawn to our attention in this book.